Help Your Child with Numeracy Ages 7–11

Also available from Continuum

Help Your Child with Numeracy Ages 3–7, Rosemary Russell

Help Your Child with Literacy Ages 3–7, Caroline Coxon

Help Your Child with Literacy Ages 7–11, Caroline Coxon

Available from Network Continuum

Help Your Boys Succeed, Gary Wilson

Help Your Child Develop Emotional Literacy, Betty Rudd

Help Your Child to Succeed, Bill Lucas and Alistair Smith

Help Your Talented Child, Barry Teare

Help Your Young Child to Succeed, Ros Bayley, Lynn Broadbent and Debbie Pullinger

Help Your Child with Numeracy Ages 7–11

Rosemary Russell

Continuum International Publishing Group
The Tower Building, 11 York Road, London SE1 7NX
80 Maiden Lane, Suite 704, New York, NY 10038

www.continuumbooks.com

British Library Cataloguing-in-Publication Data
A catalogue record for this book is available from the British Library.

ISBN: 9781847064127 (paperback)

Library of Congress Cataloging-in-Publication Data
A catalog record for this book is available from the Library of Congress.

Designed and typeset by Kenneth Burnley, Wirral, Cheshire
Printed and bound in Great Britain by Ashford Colour Press Ltd

Contents

Introduction

Maths is good for you!

Research has shown that:

- Numeracy exercises are very good for the brain
- In the long term, this helps employment prospects
- Maths qualifications can lead to more earning power.

How this book will help

This book will explain some of the milestones children make between the ages of 7 and 11 years old.

It is not a text book! It will:

- Secure your own knowledge
- Show you what schools are trying to do
- Give you ideas of how to help
- Provide exercises (Workouts!) to do with your child
- Lead you to more resources.

Moving on

This book builds on *Help Your Child with Numeracy Ages 3–7*, and often refers back to it. Some things – especially in this introduction – are repeated because they are true at any stage in a child's education; others are repeated because they are the foundations of the subject and it is so important to make sure your child has got them right before trying to move on.

Another reason for repeating things is that Key Stage 2 (i.e. ages 7–11 years old) is the time when your child will start to learn formal methods for handling the same ideas that have already been introduced informally. These formal methods of addition, subtraction, multiplication and division, dealt with in Chapter 5, are probably the most recognizable part of the syllabus as far as adults are concerned; they need some patience, because adults easily forget how long it actually took them to become familiar with these processes when they were young!

Chapter 5 is the biggest chapter in the book, but there is more to maths than doing calculations. Your child will be exploring a lot of other things that build up together into a fascinating subject, so make sure you take a good look at the other chapters as well.

The most important help – providing the right environment

One of the things that is true at any stage in a child's education is that, as a parent, your love, care and support has possibly the biggest positive influence on your child's achievement. You can help in this way even if you think (probably wrongly) that you are 'rubbish' at maths. Make sure they have a good diet, which includes fruit and vegetables, and are getting enough sleep. Let them enjoy a mixture of social activities. Have a laugh with them. Organize trips out like going swimming, visiting places of interest or going to the theatre. Having this balance is important, especially during exam times when they are older.

Everyday maths

Making maths part of everyday life is one of the best ways for children to feel confident in using and working with numbers and shapes.

For example, look out for sequences in patterns on curtains, fabrics and wallpapers. Being able to predict when the pattern next occurs helps mathematical thinking.

Practise matching objects and getting over the concept 'same as': Please fetch me a spoon the same as this. Use words which communicate comparisons: Which is the tallest/shortest tree?

For older children, shopping gives many opportunities for practising numeracy skills. Look out for offers: Buy two get the third free. Work out with them how much each item costs, and how much has been saved.

Start from where they are

Be sensitive when a child gets something wrong. Don't just say, 'You've got that wrong, this is how you do it.' Instead, start from where they're at and ask them, 'Tell me, how did you get that answer?' As they discuss things with

you, areas of misunderstanding and so on will become clear. Then show them where they went wrong, and help them to correct the mistake.

Often, they have misunderstood or half-learnt a procedure, or they do not understand certain mathematical words or symbols (see the glossary at the back of the book). It could be that they have just misread the question!

Lots of ways to learn

There is no single, exclusively correct learning style in maths. We learn things in a variety of ways, so help children to learn by using two or more of their senses, e.g. hearing as well as seeing. Children can make use of a multisensory approach to learning multiplication facts (tables):

- Write out tables
- Draw arrays or groups of objects
- Learn tables to a rhythm or rap
- Cover the tables over
- Write down the multiplication facts
- Check what you have written.

Some of the methods used to teach the basics such as addition, subtraction, multiplication and division may come as a surprise. Hopefully this book will help you to recognize what is going on, and the thinking behind it, so you can work alongside school, and not confuse your child. If you are unsure, do ask the teacher.

Keep in touch with the teacher, and don't be afraid to discuss any concerns you may have. Remember to pass on any good news too!

Praise and encouragement – building self-esteem

It is tremendously important to praise what is right, and not focus only on mistakes. If there has been a lot of failure at maths, a child's self-esteem can be brought down and this does not help them to learn. So, encourage them to ask questions if they don't understand, and reassure them that no question is too simple to ask. They may need another type of explanation, so be ready to give that. Remind them that other people probably have the same problem, but don't have the courage to ask. If they get stuck, backtrack to the point where they did understand, and start from there. Build self-esteem by encouraging them that these are quite common experiences. The key is to celebrate what is right!

Great expectations – but not too great!

Good maths is built on solid foundations, and these take time to settle. It is very important to develop mental arithmetic skills, even though calculators do exist. Be patient. Be aware that there is a huge gap between the very important early stages of informal, mental arithmetic and the formal, written methods that adults expect to see. Don't try to jump too quickly!

Note that many of the *Workouts* in this book indicate the school year in which children will meet that work.

Using practice books can be helpful, as long as sessions are not too long and the tasks are appropriate for the child's age.

Remember that children learn at different rates.

Schools

National Curriculum

The National Curriculum describes what children are to be taught. It applies to all students of compulsory school age in maintained schools in England.

Key Stages

The National Curriculum is organized broadly into what are known as Key Stages. The pupils' ages dictates which Key Stage they belong to. A rough guide to the ages is as follows:

Key Stage 1	5–7 years old	Year groups 1–2
Key Stage 2	7–11 years old	Year groups 3–6
Key Stage 3	11–14 years old	Year groups 7–9
Key Stage 4	14–16 years old	Year groups 10–11

Numeracy Strategy (The Primary Framework for Mathematics)

In September 1999, the Government introduced in primary schools the National Numeracy Strategy to help raise standards in mathematics for all primary-aged pupils. The National Curriculum says *what* is to be taught, whereas the 'Strategy' (or 'Framework') gives guidance on *how* mathematics is to be taught. This Strategy was further streamlined in September 2007. From September 2007, mathematics in primary schools is considered under seven main headings, or 'strands'. They are:

- Using and applying mathematics
- Counting and understanding number
- Knowing and using number facts
- Calculating
- Understanding shape
- Measuring
- Handling data.

The table below shows the sorts of things children learn, and how they relate to these seven strands.

These 'strands' are very much an adult guide to the teaching of the subject, and children will probably be completely unaware of them. They will be our guide to breaking down the subject in this book but, like the strands of a rope, they run in parallel throughout the course and are closely bound together. There is a great deal of overlap and they all work to reinforce each other. Any one topic, or even any one lesson, might involve several strands.

Strands	**Examples of things most children learn**
Using and applying mathematics	How to solve problems involving everyday situations. *E.g. Exchanging foreign currency. How many US dollars would John get for £70? (Year 5). This is an example of a one-step calculation.*
Counting and understanding number	Place value and how to put decimals in the correct order. *E.g. Put these lengths in order, starting with the smallest first: 1.3 m, 2.1 m, 1.7 m and 2.3 m (Year 4).*

	How to make an estimate and how to round numbers. *E.g. 6487 people attended a football match. What is that to the nearest 1000? 100? 10? (Year 5).*
Knowing and using number facts	Children learn their 'times tables' up to 10 × 10. As well as multiplication they learn division facts too. *(Please see grid in Appendix 1.)* Children learn addition and subtraction facts too. *For example, by the end of Year 3, it is useful to know by heart all the addition and subtraction facts for all numbers up to, and including 20.* *E.g, Know the pairs for 11:* *1 + 10 = 11 10 + 1 = 11 2 + 9 = 11 9 + 2 = 11, etc.* *11 – 1 = 10 11 – 10 = 1 11 – 2 = 9 11 – 9 = 2, etc.*
Calculating	Understanding when to carry out a division or a multiplication. *For example, 'share 55 sweets between 5 friends' involves calculating a division (Year 4). Whereas, 'find the product of 75 and 4' involves calculating a multiplication (Year 4).* Shortcuts to mental calculations. *Here, knowing doubling is very useful. For example, multiplying by 4 is the same as doubling and doubling again. So 16 x 4 is the same as double 16 (32) then double again (64).* How to write out calculations formally, known as 'Pencil and Paper Procedures'. *For example, at first, additions sums are simple and written out in a line. The next stage is to learn how to write them in a vertical layout, and do the calculation. Children are asked first how they* ***mentally*** *work out the calculation, and try to write that down.* *E.g. 74 + 58 = (70 + 50) + (4 + 8) = 120 + 12 = 132 or* *74 + 58 = (4 + 8) + (70 + 50) = 12 + 120 = 132*

Children gradually move to a vertical format, and by the end of Year 3, have moved towards 'carrying' below the line.

E.g.

$$\begin{array}{r} 57 \\ +\,26 \\ \hline 83 \\ {\scriptstyle 1} \end{array}$$

Children are introduced to using calculators as a tool to carry out calculations in about Year 5, though some may have used one earlier for special things like, for instance, exploring sequences of numbers.

Understanding shape	Here children learn that a whole turn is 360° (Year 4). They learn how to use a protractor to measure and draw angles (Year 5), and how to calculate angles in a triangle (Year 6). They are gradually introduced to more types of 2-D and 3-D shapes. They classify shapes by their properties. *For example, in Year 3 they learn that a hemisphere is a sphere cut in half. The shape of the flat surface is a circle.*
Measuring	How to read and use timetables using a 24-hour clock (Year 5). In Year 4 they start to explore area and perimeters. They learn the word perimeter, and what it means. *For example, draw around the edge of a rectangle. How far is it? This distance is the perimeter.* They calculate the area and perimeter of squares and rectangles, using a formula (Year 5).
Handling data	Children learn how to organize information (data) into a form that is easier to understand, so that decisions can be made. They learn about the probability (likelihood) of an event occurring (Year 5) and then how to predict an event occurring (Year 6). They learn about averages. They use the mode (Year 5) to summarize data. In Year 6, they use the mean and median to describe data.

Numeracy Hour

In some primary schools, each day schoolchildren spend about an hour (between 45 and 60 minutes, depending on their age) learning mathematics, and so their lessons are often known as the Numeracy Hour.

There is a lot of emphasis on mental calculations at first. Once these are secure, children are introduced to standard written methods. Using the correct mathematical vocabulary is important too.

Typical lessons

Their lessons are usually split into three parts:

The oral/mental starter: this lasts approximately 10 minutes, and the children are taught together. It is time to practise skills.

The main teaching activity: this lasts about 30–40 minutes. Children may work in groups for this part.

The plenary: the last 10 minutes or so are spent with the whole class together, discussing and finding out what the children have learnt. The teacher might also use this time to remind students of the important points of the lesson.

SATs and assessment

Throughout the year teachers are continually assessing students to monitor their progress and use the information to help plan suitable work. When children are about 7 and 11 years old, those who attend maintained schools in England are required to take tests, commonly known as SATs.

Although at Key Stage 1 the teacher has quite a lot of flexibility in setting the test and does the marking, at Key Stage 2 (for children aged approximately 11) these tests are taken in May and are sent off to be externally marked.

The children's results are given in the form of a level (see below). You will be sent a report informing you what level your child is working at.

Levels

Each 'level' roughly describes what sort of things a child is capable of doing in a particular subject. They start at Level 1 and work upwards. So to be at Level 3, a child would have to progress through Level 1 and Level 2, which may be further split into sections which start at 2c, then 2b and 2a. Most children by the age of 7 are working at Level 2, and most children by the age of 11 are working at Level 4.

Remember, do not worry if they seem ahead in some areas and not so strong in others. Children learn at different rates.

Using and applying mathematics

Background

Mathematics provides many tools to solve problems in everyday situations. One of the main aspects of this strand is about recognizing which tool you need and learning how to apply it.

There are many skills associated with problem solving and in this section we will discuss tips that will help you to help your child.

One typical situation that affects all of us is solving problems associated with money. We will use money problems as examples, but the underlying principles can be used for problems to do with measures and time.

Strategies to help

Break down the problem into simple steps

Many problems look complicated but are really only a sequence of simple operations. It is important to recognize the steps in a calculation, and encourage your child to break them down into single steps, and solve each part.

One-step, two-step and multi-step problems

Look at these questions:

1. A fairground ride costs 80p for a child. How much does it cost for 2 children?

2. A fairground ride costs 80p for a child. How much change is left if 2 children go on the ride and pay with a £5 note.

The first question involves only one calculation, a multiplication, to get the answer £1.60. This is an example of a one-step problem.

However, the second question involves first using a multiplication to find the cost of the entrance for 2 (that's one step) and then finding the change from £5, calculating a subtraction (the second step) to give the answer £3.40. Here we have an example of a two-step problem.

Children solve one-step and two-step problems in about Year 3.

Let's look at another example:

3. If you were to go shopping for the best buy of a particular item in a sale, and you calculated the sale price and compared sale prices in different shops, then that would be an example of a multi-step problem. Let's break them down and see the steps:

   (i) Calculate the discount (step one)

   (ii) Find the discounted price (step two)

   (iii) Do this in other shops (each involves two steps)

   (iv) Then compare the prices by placing them in order (step three)

   (v) Make the decision on what is the lowest price to find the best buy (step four).

Understand what the problem is about

In a test, it might help children to underline key words, and pieces of information. In our first example, the cost for each (80p) is important, and *how much does it cost 2 children* is what you are being asked. So I recommend underlining these.

Understand what calculations are required

In our multi-step question, there are several mathematical skills required.

How to calculate a percentage; how to calculate the discounted price (here, subtract the discount). Do this for all shops you are looking at. Put the prices in order (ordering decimals), this enables you to see the least price.

There is nothing difficult about this, but we can see that it is important to know when to, and how to, use the appropriate calculation.

How you can help your child

As children progress through the years, they meet problems that make use of the skills they are acquiring. You can help by discussing with them their methods and talking about how to solve problems in other areas such as time and measures.

Counting and understanding number

The strands overlap a great deal. Some topics (marked*) in this chapter are technically part of the *Calculating* strand but are dealt with here for convenience.

Background

Our number system is a very simple, clever and elegant structure that allows us to write down very complicated arithmetic with very few symbols. Understanding how it works is the key to everything.

We can all carry some simple calculations in our heads and these may enable us to 'get by', up to a point, without really understanding what is going on. Some children have a remarkable ability to bluff and blag their way through for quite a while – or perhaps just to hide the simple misery of stumbling blindly in a sea of numbers. If a child of any age is having difficulty with arithmetic – the basic processes of adding, subtracting, multiplying and dividing – it is worth checking whether they really do understand what a number stands for.

So, just to be sure, let us start at the very beginning. And remember: a good supply of pennies, 10p coins and £1 (100p) coins and perhaps even a £10 (1000p) note makes a very good visual aid for getting to grips with this subject.

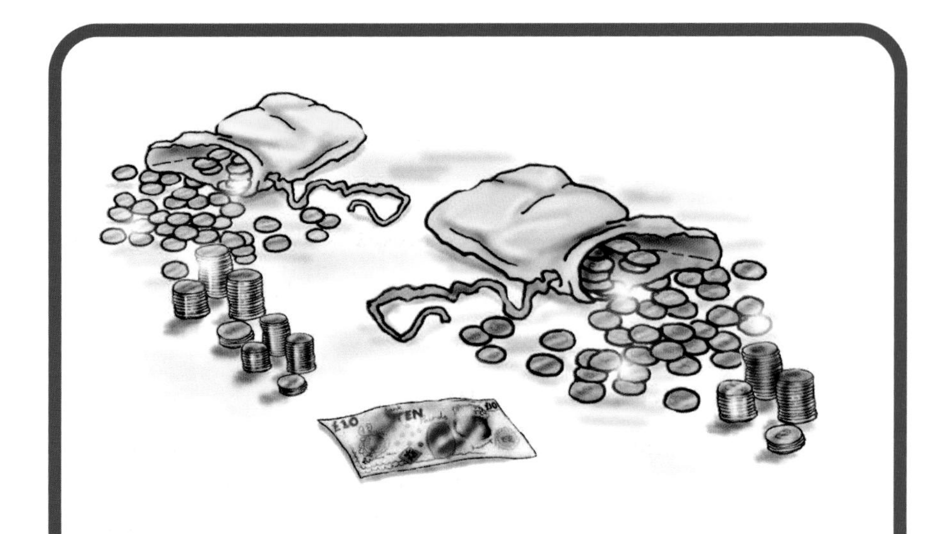

Units, tens, hundreds and thousands: how our number system works

We arrange our numbers in tens. We begin counting things with the digits 1, 2, 3, 4, 5, 6, 7, 8 and 9, and these are called Units. After nine, we say 'ten' and write it as 10; the 1 on the left means one group of Ten and the 0 ('nought' or 'zero') on the right shows that there are no Units.

The next number is eleven: 1 Ten and 1 Unit, 11. We then go up through the Units again: 12, 13, 14 . . . up to 19. After 19 we have twenty: 2 Tens and 0 Units, 20. So we go on until we get to 99; after this, we have 10 Tens (which we call a Hundred), no other Tens and no Units, 100.

The beauty of it is that we can keep on doing this indefinitely: every time we reach ten, we can start a new column to the left. So with only ten digits (0–9) we can write down any number, no matter how big. The position of each digit tells us how much it is worth: this is its **Place Value**.

An extract from our number system

Thousands	Hundreds	Tens	Units
(1000)	(100)	(10)	(1)
	8	0	5
2	0	3	0

The number eight hundred and five would be written as 8 in the hundreds column, there are no tens (i.e. no twenty, thirty etc.) so zero is placed in the tens column, and there are five units so 5 is placed in the units column.

$8 \times 100 \quad = \quad 800$

$0 \times 10 \quad = \quad 0$

$5 \times 1 \quad = \quad 5$

Adding together gives:

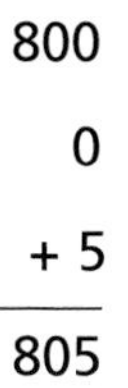

In the number two thousand and thirty, there are two thousands, so 2 is placed in the thousands column, no hundreds so zero is placed in the hundreds column, thirty (which is three tens) is represented by 3 in the tens column, and no units so zero is placed in the units column. (See table above.)

In any whole number, the value of the units column must be shown (even if it is zero). From its position we can work out the value of all the other digits.

Rewriting a number in smaller units

An important numeracy skill is to be able to rewrite a number in smaller units. Here are some examples. ONE hundred is the same as TEN tens, or ONE HUNDRED units. So 500 is the same as fifty tens (ten tens equals one hundred, so twenty tens equals two hundred . . . so fifty tens equals five hundred). ONE thousand is TEN hundreds.

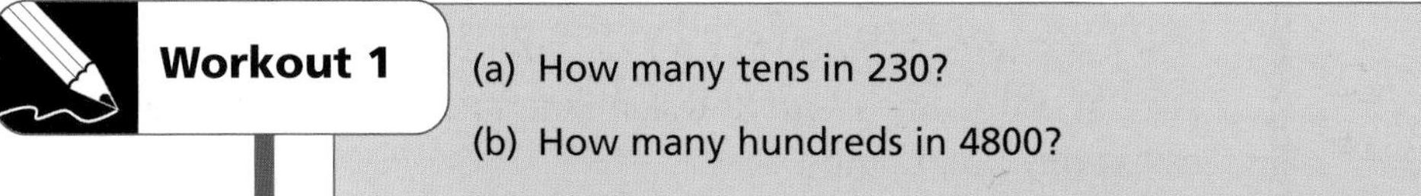

Workout 1

(a) How many tens in 230?

(b) How many hundreds in 4800?

(c) Which is more, 81 tens or 8 hundreds? (Year 4)

Starting off

Children start off by learning that numbers are used to identify, for example, how many books there are on a shelf: in other words, how many particular objects are present. It is important that they are not just reciting by heart.

Gradually they extend their knowledge into 100s, learning to read and write two-digit and three-digit numbers in figures as well as words by the end of Year 2, and at least 1000 by the end of Year 3.

Decimals

As children progress through primary school, their knowledge of the number system increases too. They realize that we need to describe amounts that are not whole numbers, (for example half a chocolate bar; discussed later in the section on fractions), and that there are numbers that are between whole numbers, called decimals.

Decimal fractions, to give them their full name, are fractions with denominators 10, 100, 1000, etc. We use a special notation to write these fractions, called decimal notation, and write

$$\frac{1}{10} \text{ as } 0.1, \quad \frac{1}{100} \text{ as } 0.01, \text{ etc.}$$

Thanks to the elegant simplicity of our number system, there is no difficulty in slotting into it these numbers (or parts of numbers) less than one. Just as we can make bigger and bigger numbers by extending the system to the left, beyond Thousands to Tens of Thousands, Hundreds of Thousands, Millions and so on, so we can extend the system to the right of the units column to make smaller and smaller numbers. The same logic applies throughout: the value of each place (column) is ten times that of the next place to the right. All that is required is the Decimal Point (.) to show where the whole number ends and the decimals begin.

Thousands	Hundreds	Tens	Units .	Tenths	Hundredths
(1000)	(100)	(10)	(1) .	($\frac{1}{10}$ = 0.1)	($\frac{1}{100}$ = 0.01)

Money is again an invaluable visual aid and shopping is an excellent way to introduce children to decimals. They can see the price of things being whole pounds, and parts of a pound. If the item costs £7.42, point out that it means 7 whole pounds plus some more. The cost is between £7 and £8.

Note that 7p is written as £0.07 – you must have the first 0 because you always show the Units, then you have the decimal point, then the second 0 because there are no Tenths, so that the 7 appears in the correct place.

Measuring using metric measurements such as metres is another way of introducing decimals to children.

Multiplying and dividing by 10, 100, 1000*

By the end of Year 4, most students learn how to multiply and divide numbers, up to 1000, by 10 and 100. Let's look at the numbers 81, 810 and 8100 to gain an understanding of the process.

Thousands	Hundreds	Tens	Units .	Tenths	Hundredths
(1000)	(100)	(10)	(1) .	($\frac{1}{10}$ = 0.1)	($\frac{1}{100}$ = 0.01)
		8	1		
	8	1	0		
8	1	0	0		

When we multiply by 10, we are making every part of the number '81' ten times bigger. So,

$$81 \times 10 = (80 \times 10) + (1 \times 10)$$
$$= 800 + 10$$
$$= 810$$

This is the same as moving all the digits to **the left one space**, and putting a zero in the units column. This is because the value of the units column must be shown, even if it is zero. It holds the place value for the other digits.

If we multiply again by 10, we are making every part of the number '810' ten times larger. So,

$$810 \times 10 = (800 \times 10) + (10 \times 10) + (0 \times 10)$$
$$= (8000) + (100) + 0$$
$$= 8100$$

Combining the two calculations, we can see that

$$81 \times 10 \times 10 = 81 \times 100 = 8100$$

is the same as shifting all the digits in 81 two places to the left. We have put in the zeros to hold the place value.

Multiplying decimals by 10, 100, 1000*

We can use the same logic of shifting digits to the left for multiplying decimals by 10s, 100s etc. For example,

$$8.1 \times 10 = 81$$

We have just moved all the digits one place to the left. There is no need to add any zeros, as the value of the units column is shown. Another example is:

$$1.415 \times 10 = 14.15$$

If when carrying out a decimal multiplication by 10, or 100, or 1000 etc. the units column were to become blank, we would then put in a zero in the units column, as usual, to hold the place value of the other digits. For example,

$$2.8 \times 100 = 280$$

Division by 10, 100, 1000*

Multiplication and division are inverse operations (see Glossary for explanation).

Using the same logic, we can see that dividing a number by 10 means that we move all the digits one place to the right, and dividing by 100 means we move all the digits two places to the right.

So, starting with 2075, we have

$(2075 \div 10)$ is 207.5, and

$(2075 \div 100)$ is 20.75

We need to remember to fill in zeros in columns that are empty and are required to show the place value of the remaining digits.

Here is an example:

$3 \div 100 = 0.03$

We need the zeros to show the units column, and to show that the 3 has a value of 3 hundredths.

By Year 6, most children would have learnt how to multiply a decimal fraction, with one or two decimal places, by 10 and 100, e.g. $4.52 \times 10 = 45.2$; $1.7 \times 100 = 170$. There is no need to put in the decimal point and following zero here.

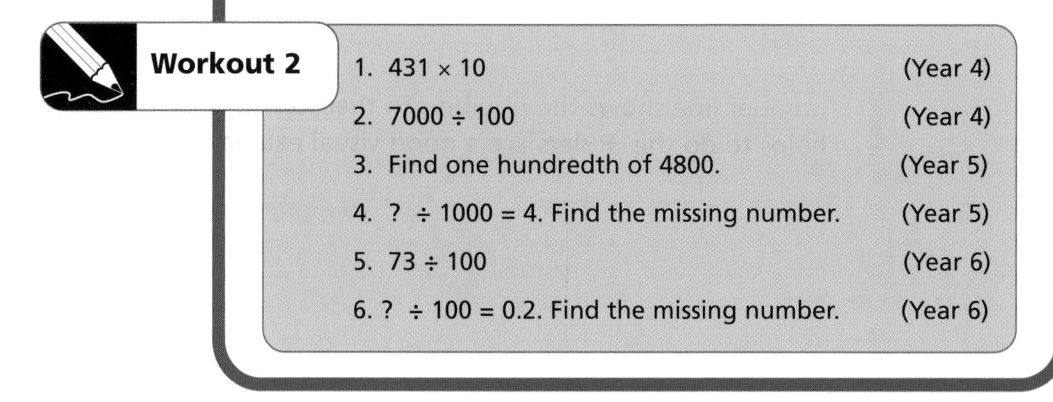

Workout 2

1. 431×10 (Year 4)
2. $7000 \div 100$ (Year 4)
3. Find one hundredth of 4800. (Year 5)
4. $? \div 1000 = 4$. Find the missing number. (Year 5)
5. $73 \div 100$ (Year 6)
6. $? \div 100 = 0.2$. Find the missing number. (Year 6)

Useful mental arithmetic skills

Knowing how to multiply 10s, 100s and 1000s, and knowing how to divide by 10s, 100s and 1000s, together with halving and doubling, are powerful mental arithmetic tools.

In Year 4 most children learn things like: to multiply by 5, firstly multiply by 10, and then halve:

$$16 \times 5 = 16 \times (10 \div 2) = (16 \times 10) \div 2 = (160) \div 2 = 80$$

$$15 \times 20 = 15 \times 10 \times 2 = (15 \times 10) \times 2 = 300$$

In Year 5 most children extend these principles and learn things like:

$$28 \times 50 = 28 \times (100 \div 2) = 1400$$

In Year 6, most children learn things like:

$$28 \times 25 = 28 \times (100 \div 4) = 2800 \div 4 = 700$$

Workout 3

1. Half of 70 (Year 3)
2. 18×5 (Year 4)
3. 17×20 (Year 4)

Ordering numbers and the symbols > and <

It is very important to be able to order numbers. Seeing a number line shows the numbers in their correct order and helps to do this. Rulers are a good visual example of a number line.

By the end of Year 4, most children have learnt to use the symbols for 'greater than', **>**, and 'less than', **<**. For example, $5 > 3$ and $2 < 6$.

Counting in different steps

Children will have had plenty of practice of counting on from and back down to zero, in steps of different sizes by the end of Year 4. A good way to help is to practise counting in different steps with your child. For example, start at 6.2, and then count on in steps of one tenth. Try counting back down too (Year 4).

Negative numbers

By the end of Year 4, they will have met negative numbers, for example in real life situations such as reading temperatures from a thermometer. And so, by the end of Year 5, they would meet an activity where they would be counting back through zero, in steps of 4, and need to continue the sequence:

Nine, five, one, negative three, negative seven . . .

Please note: in common usage, some people may say, 'minus three, minus seven . . .'; the sequence is written as 9, 5, 1, –3, –7, . . .

Making connections – sequences

3, 1, –1, –3, –5 . . .

Children may also be asked to find the rule for a sequence and fill in missing members of a sequence. For example, when we look at the above sequence, can you see there is a pattern to it? Can you explain what is the connection between each 'term' and the next in the list? Can you predict what is the next number?

Starting at 3, to find the next member of the sequence we subtract two. The rule is: to find the next member of the sequence, we subtract two from the current member. The next number is –7.

Workout 4

1. Fill in the next three numbers in this sequence

   52, 47, 42, . . . , . . . , . . . (Year 4)

2. What are the missing numbers in this sequence? Can you explain the rule?

   . . . , . . . , 37, 40, . . . , 46, 49 (Year 4)

3. What is the rule for this sequence? Fill in the next three numbers

   –25, –22, –19, . . . , . . . , . . . (Year 5)

4. Explain the rule, and give the next two terms

   5, 19, . . . , . . . , 61, . . . , . . . (Year 6)

Ordering decimals

By the end of Year 4, children are using decimal notation, and placing decimals in order.

The skill of ordering decimals is very important in everyday life, particularly when it comes to calculations involving measurement and money. For example, we may want to make a decision about which item is cheaper. In that case, once we have put the prices in order, so that we can compare like with like, we would choose the least value.

Workout 5

1. Write as a decimal fraction (i) six tenths (ii) forty-eight and seven tenths. (Year 4)
2. Which is lighter (i) 4.8 kg or 6.8 kg (ii) 3.82 kg or 3.28 kg? (Year 4)
3. Place in order, on a line from 8.9 to 9.1: 8.95, 9.04, 8.92, 9.09, 8.98. (Year 5)
4. Which is less, £6.40 or £6.04? (Year 4)

Fractions, decimals and percentages

Fractions, decimals and percentages are all ways of describing parts of a whole. In everyday life, we use the word fraction to mean something smaller. For example, 'I bought this belt at a fraction of the price' – means that you have got a bargain, and paid a smaller price than usual. Fractions have a similar meaning in mathematics except when you split something into fractions, either an item such as a cake, or an amount such as 30p, you split whatever you start with into smaller **equal** parts. Halving is splitting something into two equal parts; splitting into thirds means splitting that something into three equal parts.

Equivalent fractions

At first, children learn to recognize fractions such as ½. Later, they learn that the same fraction can be written in many ways.

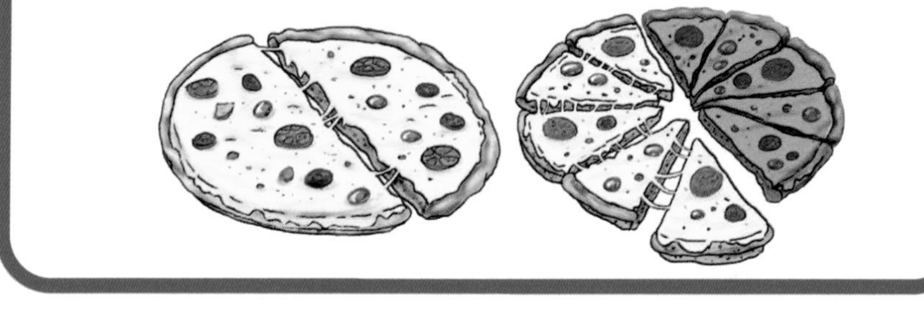

For example, look at the pizza. The one on the left is cut in half. The one on the right is cut into 10 equal parts, and five of them are shaded.

You can see that $\frac{1}{2} = \frac{5}{10}$.

$\frac{1}{2}$ and $\frac{5}{10}$ are what is known as equivalent fractions, in other words, they have the same value. (In fact, each fraction can be written in millions of equivalent ways, but children do not appreciate that until very much later on!)

In Year 3 most children learn that $\frac{1}{2} = \frac{5}{10}$, and $\frac{1}{2}$ of $\frac{1}{2} = \frac{1}{4}$.

Very practically, equivalence between fractions can be seen by doing the following:

- Take a piece of A4 paper. Fold it in half.
- Open it up. Count the number of parts (2).
- Now fold the paper into quarters (fold in half, then fold in half again).
- Open it up. You can see that $\frac{1}{2} = \frac{2}{4}$ (Year 2).

As children progress, they learn more about equivalent fractions,

e.g. $\frac{2}{8} = \frac{1}{4}$

and $\frac{4}{8} = \frac{2}{4} = \frac{1}{2}$ (Year 4).

They extend their knowledge into different types of fractions, such as tenths and fifths,

e.g. $\frac{4}{10} = \frac{2}{5}$ (Year 4).

This knowledge is built on, year upon year, at Key Stage 2. Through a lot of practical work, children put fractions in order of size.

E.g. Write down any of these fractions that are less than a half:

$\frac{1}{3}$, $\frac{3}{4}$, $\frac{1}{10}$. (Year 4) (Answer: $\frac{1}{3}$ and $\frac{1}{10}$).

As you can see, we use special symbols to show a fraction.

Finding a fraction of an amount*

A half is written as $\frac{1}{2}$. The bottom number (the denominator) tells you the number of equal parts that make a whole, and the top number (the numerator) tells you how many of these equal parts you have. So using our example, halving a cake means splitting the cake into two, each piece is $\frac{1}{2}$ a cake.

Halving 30p would mean splitting the 30p into two, and each half would be 15p.

Taking this a step further, we can find $\frac{2}{3}$ of 30p. We know from the denominator we need to split the amount into 3 equal parts, so $\frac{1}{3}$ of 30p is 10p. We want $\frac{2}{3}$ so two of these equal parts gives a total of 20p.

Workout 6

Find $\frac{1}{3}$ of (i) 15 (ii) 6 (iii) 24. (Year 4)

Find $\frac{3}{10}$ of (i) 70 (ii) 40 (iii) 90. (Year 5)

Find $\frac{7}{10}$ of 3 metres in centimetres. (Year 6)

Decimal fractions

1000 etc. are known as decimals or decimal fractions, and a special notation is used to write these fractions, called decimal notation, as has been mentioned before. Children are introduced to decimals in about Year 4. They learn about the equivalence between decimals and fractions, and how the basic ones can be interchanged.

E.g. $\frac{1}{2} = \frac{5}{10} = 0.5$

$\frac{1}{4} = 0.25$ $\quad$ $0.75 = \frac{3}{4}$

This is where taking practical measurements can be very helpful to see the connections, and parents can help enormously.

Percentages

Another way we can express parts of a whole is by the use of percentages. As the name suggests, percentages are to do with 'hundreds' (*cent* is Latin for hundred).

The whole of something is said to be, 'one hundred per-cent'. We write this as 100%; half is 50%, one quarter is 25%.

Children are introduced to percentages in about Year 5.

They learn and recognize that: $10\% = 0.1 = \frac{1}{10}$.

Finding a percentage of an amount

Percentages can be written as fractions in which the denominator is 100. So to find 10% of £30 we want $\frac{10}{100}$ of it, which is the same as finding $\frac{1}{10}$. Divide £30 by 10 to give the answer £3.

Recognizing the equivalence between percentages and fractions is very useful. Children can mentally find percentages of an amount, by using halving and quartering, and dividing by 10 and 100.

For example, find 12½% of £84.

Here we can use halving and quartering. Since 50% is one half, we can find 50% of £84 by dividing by 2.

50% of £84 = £42 (50% is one half, so divide £84 by 2)

25% of £84 = £21 (half of 50%). Now, 12½% is half of 25%, so we need to find half of £21.

The final answer, 12½% of £84 = £10.50.

Once you have mastered the skills of doubling and halving, a calculation like this is done mentally, very speedily!

Workout 7

1. Find 25% of £140. (Year 5)
2. Find 40% of £15. (Year 6)
3. Find 12½% of £24,000. (Year 6)

Ratio and proportion

Students are introduced to the concepts of ratio and proportion in about Year 4, by the use of phrases such as '*in every*' and '*for every*'. This topic can be slightly confusing because the words 'ratio' and 'proportion' represent two quite different ways of looking at the same thing; and, although we probably use the two concepts daily and quite correctly in everything from politics to mixing a glass of squash, the language we use in casual conversation tends to be very mixed up; many people would find it difficult to say what the difference is between 'ratio' and 'proportion' even though they would never confuse the concepts. The real key is in the use of phrases such as, *'in every'*, and *'for every'*.

Look at this string of beads; there are two types of bead, white and black.

You could say: 1 *in every* 4 beads is white (or, 2 *in every* 8 beads are white; etc.).

So the fraction of white beads is ¼. Here, we are comparing one part to the whole: this is a 'proportion'.

The terms proportion and fraction are more or less interchangeable. So we can say, 1 in every 4 beads is white: ¼ are white. What proportion is black? The answer is ¾.

However, you can also say: *for every* 1 white bead there are 3 black beads. Here we are comparing one part to another part: this is a 'ratio'.

So, the proportion is 1 *in* 4, while the ratio is 1 *to* 3.

A ratio is a way we compare two or more quantities. Recipes are an excellent example of the practical way we use ratio. For example, here is a list of the ingredients for a recipe of a Victoria Sponge cake:

100g margarine

100g caster sugar

200g self-raising flour

2 eggs

This recipe is a ratio.
We are comparing the quantities we need. *For every* 100g of margarine, use 100g of caster sugar etc. If we doubled the quantity of margarine used, all the other quantities would need to be doubled too.

By using expressions such as *'in every'* and *'for every'* children start to grasp the idea of ratio and proportion. They first meet this in about Year 4.

We use a colon, : , as the symbol to mean ratio, and children would start to use this in about Year 6 to Year 7.

For a Victoria Sponge cake, the ratio could be written as

Margarine: sugar: flour: eggs. And numerically,

100g: 100g: 200g: 2 eggs.

Why not try adapting a recipe for 4 to make it a recipe for 8? Cook it together with your child!

In Year 4, children learn how to estimate two-digit and then three-digit numbers, to the nearest 10 or 100, and by Year 6, they would learn how to estimate, for example, the numbers at a Premier League football match, to the nearest 10, 100, 1000 and 10,000, and how to deal with numbers in the hundreds of thousands and millions.

In Year 4, they learn that 750 rounds to 800, as it is exactly half way between 700 and 800, and so the nearest hundred to 750 is 800, as we round up when the number lies exactly half way between two hundreds.

The rule for rounding

Identify the place value digit to which you are rounding (i.e. 10, 100, 1000 etc.). Now look immediately to the right of that. If that digit is 5 or more, round up your original digit. Less than 5, keep it the same.

E.g. Round 437 to the nearest 10. The answer is 440.

4**3**7

| _______ 7 is more than 5 so round up digit in 10s column to 40

|

Place value of digit in question is 30.

Workout 9

1. Round (a) 544 (b) 947 to the nearest 10. (Year 4)
2. Round 352 to the nearest 100. (Year 4)
3. Round 7315 to the nearest 1000. (Year 5)
4. Round 2176 to the nearest 100. (Year 5)
5. Which is the best calculation for approximating 812 + 192?

   (a) 800 + 100

   (b) 900 + 200

   (c) 800 + 200

Knowing and using number facts

Mathematics is a fascinating and powerful blend of clever structures and remorseless logic that can take us to the stars. If they are to enjoy it and make the most of it, it is very important that children understand and trust how numbers work. They need to see what is happening when they add, subtract, multiply and divide, and not merely learn the subject by rote as a boring stream of apparently meaningless tables and facts.

Having said that, there should come a point when the foundations are secure and children can move on and start building on those foundations. Then it becomes important that they *do* have the facts and tables at their fingertips, as these become the building blocks for greater and more interesting things.

Knowing number facts and doubling and halving

It is very useful to know by heart all the addition and subtraction facts for all numbers up to and including 5 by the end of Year 1; up to 10 by the end of Year 2; and up to 20 by the end of Year 3.

For example, know the pairs for 11:

$1 + 10 = 11$ $10 + 1 = 11$ $2 + 9 = 11$ $9 + 2 = 11$ etc.

$11 - 1 = 10$ $11 - 10 = 1$ $11 - 2 = 9$ $11 - 9 = 2$ etc.

Using known facts to work out the addition doubles of numbers up to twenty, e.g. $17 + 17 = 34$, makes a good basis for helping with addition. It is important for children to learn addition and subtraction facts.

Learning tables

It is also important for children to learn, as well as know how to work out, multiplication and division facts too.

By the end of Year 4, the target is for children to know their 2, 3, 4, 5, 6, 7, 8, 9 and 10 times tables, up to 10 × 10, as well as the corresponding division facts.

Please see Appendix 1, which is a multiplication square showing all the times tables up to 10 × 10.

Helping your child learn their times tables is one way that parents can help enormously.

Inverse operations

Division and multiplication are what are known as inverse operations. Put simply, they 'undo' each other. Addition and subtraction are also inverse operations. First let's see how they 'undo' each other, so that we can understand an inverse operation. Children learn and use the words 'inverse operations' in about Year 4.

E.g. Starting with 4, then add 3, we get 7. But, 7 minus 3 gets us back to 4, the number we started with. The subtraction undoes the addition.

Written out, it looks like this: $4 + 3 = 7$, and $7 - 3 = 4$.

Now let's look at division and multiplication. If we start with 3 multiplied by 4 we get 12. If we divide 12 by 4 we get 3, the number we started with.

Written out, it looks like this: $3 \times 4 = 12$, and $12 \div 4 = 3$.

If you look at the multiplication square in Appendix 1, you can see how it can be used for a division as well as for a multiplication. Children would use the multiplication square and do this sort of work in about Year 5.

Estimating and checking calculations

Having learnt how to round numbers to various degrees of accuracy, children are taught how to estimate and check calculations to see if their answers are sensible and so correct. You can also check calculations by using inverse operations.

Being able to check calculations is a very important skill, especially when children start to use calculators: is that really a reasonable answer?

Using inverse operations

$537 - 78 = 459$	Check $459 + 78 = 537$ (Year 4)
Half of 34 = 17	Check double 17 = 34 (Year 4). Doubling and halving are inverse operations.
$240 \div 6 = 40$	Check $40 \times 6 = 240$

Using rounding to get an approximation

703 – 295 is approximately 700 – 300 = 400 (Year 5). Check that the answer is roughly near that. (Actual answer is 408.)

Workout 10

1. Do some checking of subtractions using inverse operations.
2. Try estimating some additions, multiplications and divisions. Check your answers by doing the actual calculation, or by using a calculator.

Calculating

Written methods

The aim is that by the end of Key Stage 2, most children will have developed efficient, reliable, compact written methods of calculation.

One of the most important ways you can help your child is to be aware of the methods used in school so that you are not taken by surprise. It means you can work together with school and so not cause confusion.

Being able to master how to calculate the basic processes of addition, subtraction, multiplication and division is one of the major skills we all need. Here is a brief outline of how these skills are taught at Key Stage 2, and some of the steps used.

Expanded	Compressed
57 + 26 = 13, 70, 83	57 + 26 = 83 (carry 1)

```
   57          57
 + 26        + 26
 ----        ----
   13          83
   70        ----
 ----          1
   83
 ----
```

There is a gradual progression. At first, no tens or hundreds need to be carried, and then calculations get more difficult. E.g. 346 + 87.

```
  346         346
 + 87        + 87
 ----        ----
   13         433
  120        ----
  300          1 1
 ----
  433
 ----
```

Before working out the sum, children are encouraged to estimate the size of their answer, and then check to see if their answer is reasonable.

Workout 11

Add these numbers using the expanded layout and the compressed layout:

(i) 58 + 35 (ii) 765 + 73

Extending addition skills to using decimals

In Year 4, children begin to extend their addition skills into adding decimals, by, for example, adding amounts of money, taking care to line up decimal points, and relevant place values.

For example, work out £2.87 + 58p.

Here we have to make sure the amounts involved are both in the same units, so change 58p into £s, i.e. £0.58. Now we can add the two amounts:

```
  £2.87
+ £0.58
  -----
  £3.45
   1 1
```

In Year 5, children's skills are extended to involve calculating with up to three decimal places, and their skills are gradually extended.

Please note: In any practical application, involving measurements of any sort, arithmetic can only make sense if the units involved are consistent. For example, a room may be 10 feet long and 2 metres wide, but to multiply 10 by 2 to get an area of '20' would be meaningless; either the 2 metres must be converted to feet to get an area in square feet, or the 10 feet must be converted to metres to get an area in square metres. Similarly, we cannot directly add kilograms to grams, or hours to minutes. Being able to convert units of measurement into the same type is an important skill and will often involve multiplying by, or dividing by 10s, 100s 1000s etc. (See 'Measuring', *How to convert between metric units*, p. 75.)

Workout 12

1. I bought a packet of pencils for £1.68 and a sharpener for 65p. What was my total bill? (Year 4)

2. In a large bowl, I add 500ml of water to 1.2 litres of water. How much water is there now in the bowl?

(Year 6)

Subtraction

When we looked at learning addition and subtraction facts, we saw that the work on subtraction is very much linked with the work on addition.

Many methods of subtraction

It is important to realize there are in fact many ways to calculate a subtraction. For example, one that is in use every day as we go about our daily lives is 'the shopkeepers' method', technically known as 'counting on' or 'complementary addition'.

When we calculate a subtraction, we are working out the gap between two numbers. You can find this gap by counting on. The answer to 11 take away 8, is the same as the answer to counting on from 8 to make 11. (Answer: 3).

An empty number line is useful to calculate this. This method is often used when giving change, and is also known as 'the shopkeepers' method'.

Another useful method is to use rounding and compensating. Here are the basic principles:

If we think of 9p as 1p less than 10p, and 99p as 1p less than £1 etc., it helps us to calculate bills quickly. We would round to the nearest pound, then compensate by taking off the extra pennies we added on at the end of the calculation.

For example,

£3.99 + £2.99 = £4 –1p + £3 – 1p = £7 – 2p = £6.98

[Please see *Help Your Child With Numeracy Ages 3–7* for more on this.]

Stages in teaching subtraction

At first, there is plenty of practice of subtraction using mental methods, number lines and jottings and rounding and compensating.

However, to cope with harder subtractions, children need to learn how to write down calculations.

Easier subtractions

At first, as with addition, subtractions are written out in lines. Children would then move to a vertical format. Beginning with numbers they can cope with mentally, they write them out in an expanded form, making sure that numbers are lined up in their correct place value. Children need to be guided to get into the habit of starting the subtraction with the units.

E.g. 86 – 53:

$$\begin{array}{r} (80 + 6) \\ -\ (50 + 3) \\ \hline (30 + 3) \end{array} = 33 \qquad \text{leads to} \quad \begin{array}{r} 86 \\ -\ 53 \\ \hline 33 \end{array}$$

or 672 – 251:

$$\begin{array}{r} (600 + 70 + 2) \\ -\ (200 + 50 + 1) \\ \hline (400 + 20 + 1) \end{array} = 421 \qquad \text{leads to} \quad \begin{array}{r} 672 \\ -\ 251 \\ \hline 421 \end{array}$$

Subtraction: the two main methods

Now, not many people know that there is more than one written method of subtracting. This can cause a lot of confusion and argument. Here are the two main methods. They are both correct, **but you must not mix them up!**

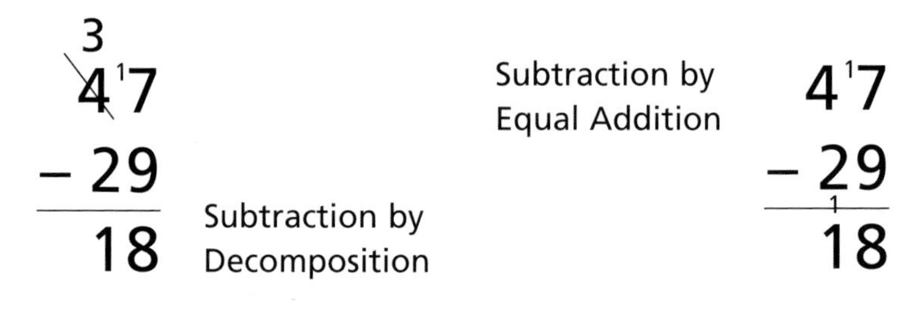

Subtraction by decomposition

The first method of subtraction is called subtraction by decomposition. This is the more commonly taught method in schools today.

We can use coins to show how to work it out.

If I have 4 × 10p and 7 × 1p coins, I have 47p; but if I have 3 × 10p and 17 × 1p coins, I also have 47p. So to solve my subtraction I can change one of my 10p coins into 10 × 1p.

$$\begin{array}{r} {\scriptstyle -1\ +10} \\ 47 \\ -\ 29 \\ \hline \end{array}$$

Seven take away nine is not possible, so . . .

$$\begin{array}{r} 3 \\ \not{4}\,{}^{1}7 \\ -\ 29 \\ \hline 18 \end{array}$$

(i) I change one of the tens in the tens column of the top number into ten units: I 'decompose' it, just like changing a ten pence piece into ten pennies.

(ii) This leaves three tens in the tens column, and we add the ten units to the units column.

(iii) Ten units plus seven makes seventeen in the units column, and nine from seventeen is eight.

(iv) In the tens column, three tens take away two tens leaves one ten.

Subtraction by equal addition

This method uses the fact that the difference between two numbers does not change if you add the same number to both. We can add 10 to each number, and the difference between 39 and 57 is just the same as the difference between 29 and 47. We can see this on the 'number line':

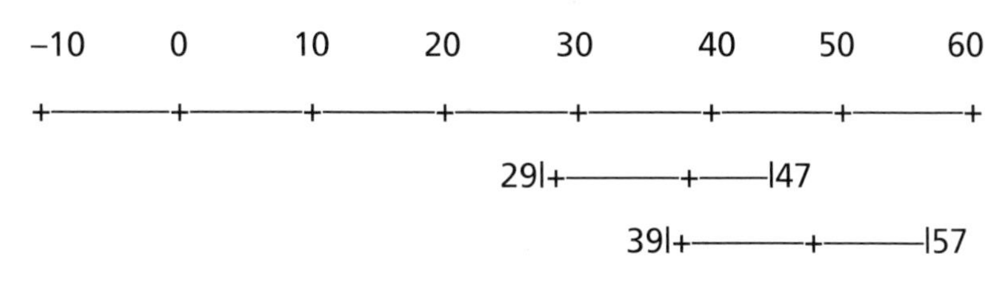

Remember that we write our numbers in columns, and each column has a value.

By adding 10 to the 29 as normal (making 39) and adding 10 to the 47 in the units column (making 57 but thinking of as it 'forty-seventeen'), we can now do the subtraction easily.

$$\begin{array}{r} 4\,{}^{1}7 \\ -\ \underset{1}{2}9 \\ \hline 18 \end{array}$$

The example on the right shows you how. 9 from 17 is 8, and 3 tens from 4 tens is 1 ten.

Workout 13

Try a subtraction involving hundreds, tens and units using the expanded method, with the vertical format beside.

How to deal with zeros when subtracting

2001 – 99 is a very simple example of a subtraction that most people would solve mentally using the 'Shopkeepers' method' of 'counting on':

99 to 100 is	1
100 to 1000 is	900
1000 to 2000 is	1000
2000 to 2001 is	1
Total	1902

However, it does make a good model to illustrate how we could perform more difficult subtractions when zeros are involved, using two different pencil and paper methods.

Decomposition

Step 1:

$$\begin{array}{r} \overset{1}{\cancel{2}}\,{}^{1}001 \\ -\quad 99 \\ \hline \end{array}$$

i. In the units column, we cannot take nine from one, so we have to get help from a column with a higher place value (i.e. to the left).

ii. The nearest column with anything in it is the Thousands; the rest have only zeros.

iii. Take one of the thousands (which leaves one behind) and change it to ten hundreds.

iv. Transfer these ten hundreds to the hundreds column. This has still not helped us with the calculation.

```
 1 9
 2¹0¹01
–   99
```

Step 2:

i. Take one of these hundreds (leaving nine behind) and change it into ten tens.

ii. Transfer these ten tens into the tens column. This still has not helped us with the calculation.

Step 3:

i. Take one of these tens (leaving nine behind) and change it to ten units.

ii. Transfer these ten units to the units column.

iii. Ten units plus one unit gives 11 units. We can now do the subtraction!

In the units column: 11 – 9 = 2.
In the tens column: 9 – 9 = 0.
In the hundreds column: 9 – 0 = 9.
In the thousands column: 1 – 0 = 1.

```
 1 9 9
 2¹0¹0¹1
–     99
    1902
```

Equal addition

Step 1: In the units column,

i. We cannot take nine from one.

ii. Add ten to the top in the units column, giving eleven units, *and* add ten to the bottom in the tens column (which shows as 1 under the tens column).

iii. In the units column, nine from eleven is two.

```
 200¹1
–   99
    ¹
     2
```

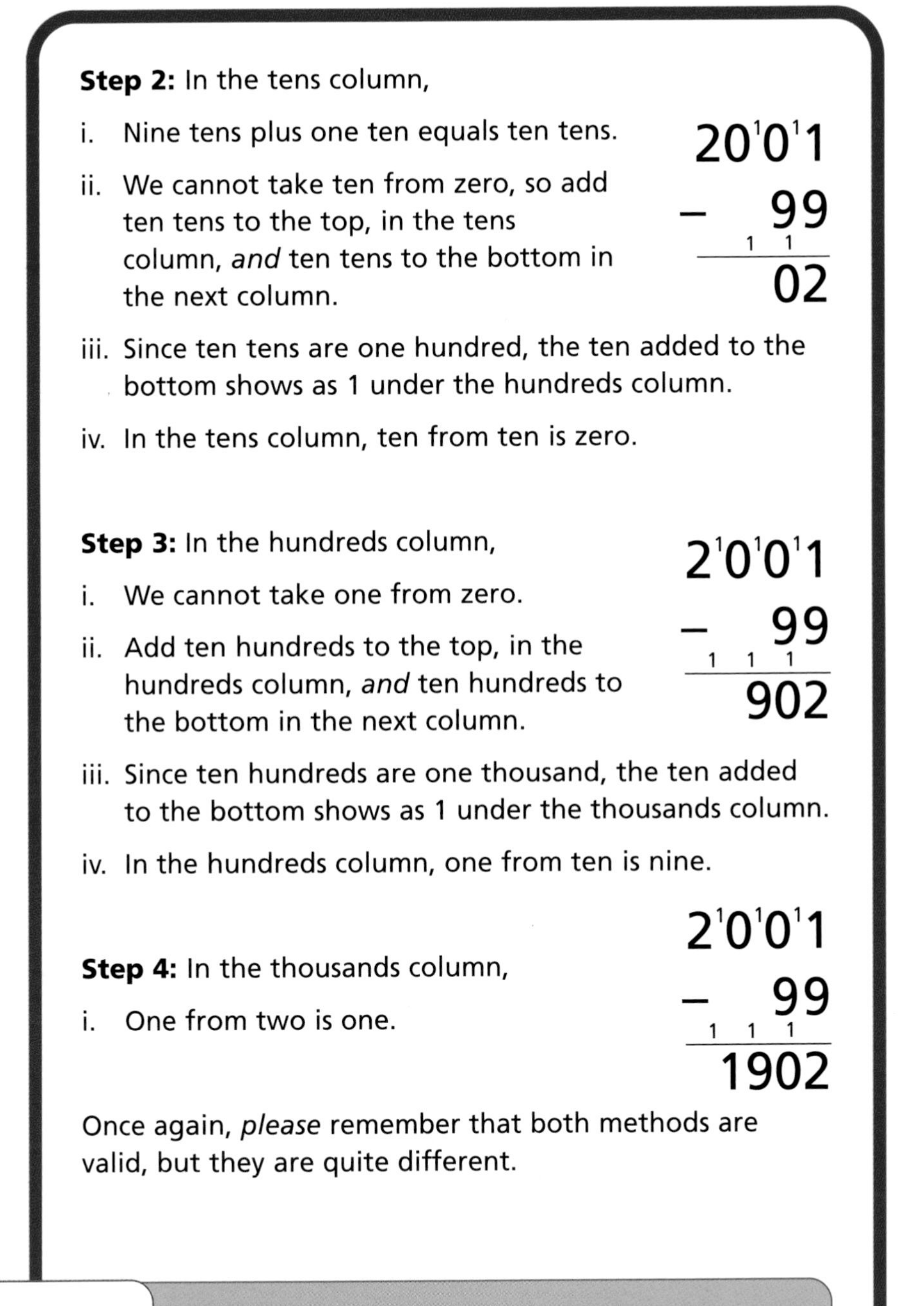

Step 2: In the tens column,

i. Nine tens plus one ten equals ten tens.

ii. We cannot take ten from zero, so add ten tens to the top, in the tens column, *and* ten tens to the bottom in the next column.

$$\begin{array}{r} 20^{1}0^{1}1 \\ -\quad 99 \\ {}^{1\ \ 1} \\ \hline 02 \end{array}$$

iii. Since ten tens are one hundred, the ten added to the bottom shows as 1 under the hundreds column.

iv. In the tens column, ten from ten is zero.

Step 3: In the hundreds column,

i. We cannot take one from zero.

ii. Add ten hundreds to the top, in the hundreds column, *and* ten hundreds to the bottom in the next column.

$$\begin{array}{r} 2^{1}0^{1}0^{1}1 \\ -\quad 99 \\ {}^{1\ \ 1\ \ 1} \\ \hline 902 \end{array}$$

iii. Since ten hundreds are one thousand, the ten added to the bottom shows as 1 under the thousands column.

iv. In the hundreds column, one from ten is nine.

Step 4: In the thousands column,

i. One from two is one.

$$\begin{array}{r} 2^{1}0^{1}0^{1}1 \\ -\quad 99 \\ {}^{1\ \ 1\ \ 1} \\ \hline 1902 \end{array}$$

Once again, *please* remember that both methods are valid, but they are quite different.

Workout 14

Try a subtraction, involving zeros, using all three methods yourself.

Subtraction using decimals

In Year 4, children extend their subtraction skills into subtracting decimals by, for example, subtracting amounts of money and lengths. They are taught to take care to line up the decimal points, so that the place values are correct. The skill of being able to change units of measurement, e.g. change 150cm into metres, is important. (Answer: 1.5 metres.)

Workout 15

1. I cut off 35cm from a rod of length 3m. How much is left? (Year 4)
2. I have £4.78 in change in my purse, and pay back the 35p I owe. How much change is left in my purse? (Year 4)

Multiplication

It is important that children understand when to carry out a multiplication. They learn in the early years that multiplication is repeated addition. They learn their multiplication facts ('times tables' up to 10 × 10). They do a lot of mental arithmetic.

However, they need to learn how to write down calculations as not all calculations can be carried out mentally.

Steps in mastering a written method of multiplication

Here are some of the steps that may be used by your child on the way to mastering a written method of multiplication.

Step 1: Mental methods using partitioning

At first, children are encouraged to use mental methods. They start learning simple tables in Year 2. They learn that it doesn't matter which way round you multiply, e.g. 6×10 is the same as 10×6. They see this through carrying out practical activities.

Then, when multiplying larger numbers, such as 34×6, they learn to partition the number into 10s and units:

$34 \times 6 = (30 \times 6) + (4 \times 6)$

They multiply the 10s:

$30 \times 6 = 180$.

And then the units:

$4 \times 6 = 24$.

And then add the totals to get the answer:

$180 + 24 = 204$

Step 2: Use of a grid

What is known as the grid or 'area' method is sometimes used in schools as the next step in mastering a written method of multiplication. It is another way of writing the same calculation, showing the steps of multiplying the tens, and the units, and then finding the total.

Here is the same calculation using the grid method.

Each number is partitioned into 10s and units. One number is put into the top row of the grid, the 10s in one cell of the grid, the units in the other cell. The second number is placed in the first column in a similar way.

Now, individually multiply together, in turn, each number in the top row, by each number in the first column, writing in the answer to this multiplication in the grid as shown. Total the results in the grid, (here the row) to get the final answer of 204.

×	30	4	
6	*180*	*24*	***204***

These are the answers to the multiplications (30 × 6) and (4 × 6).

The same calculation can be written like this too. Here we total the column to get the answers as they are the results in the grid.

×	6
30	*180*
4	*24*
	204

This is an example of TU × U (Tens and Units × Units) though teachers would probably not use this terminology with children.

Workout 16

Try using the grid method to multiply out TU × U of your choice. Make an estimate first. Check your own answer using a calculator.

Step 3: Extended grid method for TU × TU

Let's work out 53 × 27 to demonstrate how to do this.

At first, children are asked to estimate the size of the answer. Here, a rough estimate would be 50 × 30 = 1500.

The size of the grid is now increased, so that a two digit number can be multiplied by a two digit number. As before, each number is partitioned, then the multiplication is carried out systematically as before.

×	20	7
50	*1000*	*350*
3	*60*	*21*

The rows are then totalled.

×	20	7	
50	*1000*	*350*	*1350*
3	*60*	*21*	*81*

Then the two totals, at the ends of the rows, are added to find the final answer.

×	20	7	
50	*1000*	*350*	*1350*
3	*60*	*21*	*81*
			1431

Vertical format

A vertical format of the grid may be the next step used, alongside also showing the expanded working and so the link to the grid method can be seen. For example,

```
  34
×  6
----
 180  (30 × 6)
  24  (6 × 4)
----
 204
----
```

×	30	4	
6	*180*	*24*	***204***

Here is what the multiplication of 53 × 27 would look like using the vertical format, and alongside also showing the expanded working and so the link to the grid method can be seen.

```
   53
 × 27
-----
 1000  (50 × 20)
   60  (3 × 20)
  350  (50 × 7)
   21  (3 × 7)
-----
 1431
-----
```

×	20	7	
50	*1000*	*350*	*1350*
3	*60*	*21*	*81*
			1431

Step 4: Compact vertical format

At about the end of Year 5, a more compact vertical method may be used, with the expanded layout beside so that children can see the links. You can help by referring to the actual value of the digits when helping your child. This reinforces place value.

$$
\begin{array}{r l}
53 & \\
\times\ 27 & \\
\hline
1060 & (53 \times 20) \\
371 & (53 \times 7) \\
\hline
1431 & \\
\hline
\end{array}
$$

This is probably the form of long multiplication that most adults recognise, and have learnt by heart.

This calculation can be also successfully carried out by multiplying the units first, and then the tens.

Workout 17

Try using all the methods with a TU × TU of your own choice. Estimate first, and then check your final answer by using a calculator.

Division

Background

Just as with multiplication it is important that children understand what division is and when to carry out a division.

In the early years they learn about the fact that division and multiplication are inverse functions. They learn about the ways division can be seen.

One way is to see it as sharing equally. For instance, if I share 8 conkers equally between 2 people, to work out how many each gets I need to calculate a division.

$8 \div 2 = 4$

Each gets 4. Another way to see division is to see it as grouping or repeated subtraction. For example, how many groups of 2 conkers can I make from 8 conkers? You can find this out by grouping the conkers into twos. There are 4 groups. Or, by taking away 2 conkers at a time, you find there are 4 such groups.

To work this out, we calculate the division:

$8 \div 2 = 4$

[Please see *Help Your Child With Numeracy Ages 3–7* for more on this.]

Using a number line

How many groups (lots) of 6 are there in 99? In other words:

$99 \div 6$

We could keep subtracting 6's until a number less than 6 remains (the '**remainder**').

$99 - 6 - 6 - 6 \ldots - 6 = 3$

There are 16 lots of 6 in 99, with a remainder of 3, or 16 r3.

Understanding shape

Background

We are surrounded by shapes, and there is quite a lot to recognize and understand about them.

Flat surfaces, such as tops of tables, are examples of 2-D shapes. A can of baked beans and a small can of tuna are examples of 3-D shapes.

At first, children learn to distinguish 2-D and 3-D shapes according to properties. For example, they may sort a collection of 3-D shapes according to properties such as:

- Do they have corners? (E.g. cubes)
- Are all the edges straight?

Children are gradually introduced to more types of 2-D and 3-D shapes, and learn the names of the shapes.

Angles

One very important aspect of understanding shape is how to recognize and measure angles. One way we measure angles is in degrees. The symbol for a degree is °. By about the end of Year 4, most children have learnt that a whole turn is 360°. Angles measure parts of a turn. It is important to recognize that a ½ turn is 180°; that a ¼ turn is 90°, and this is also known as a 'right angle'; and ½ a right angle is 45°.

Types of angles

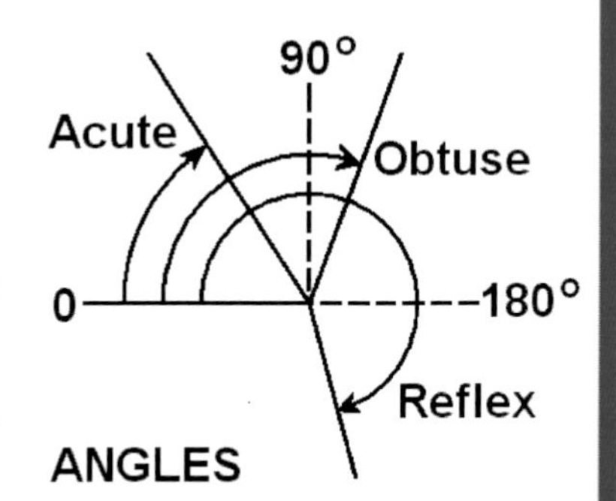

Children learn that

- Angles less than 90° are called acute angles (Year 5)
- Angles over 90° but less than 180° are called obtuse (Year 5)
- An angle that is greater than 180° but less than 360° is called a reflex angle (Year 6).

It is an important skill to recognize the differences between the types of angles, and you can help in this by discussing angle types in objects in everyday situations.

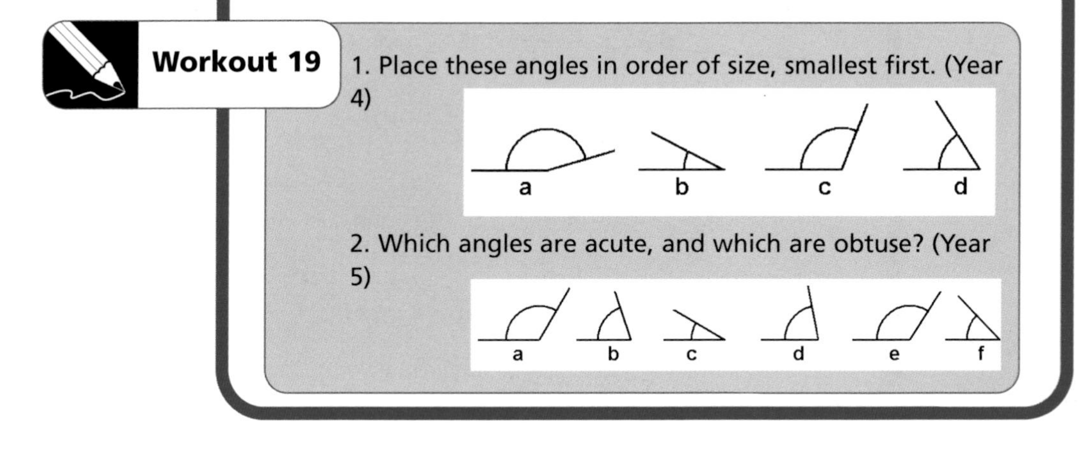

Workout 19

1. Place these angles in order of size, smallest first. (Year 4)

2. Which angles are acute, and which are obtuse? (Year 5)

Measuring angles

We measure angles using a protractor. Most children start to learn how to use a protractor in about Year 5 to measure angles, and draw them.

How to use a protractor

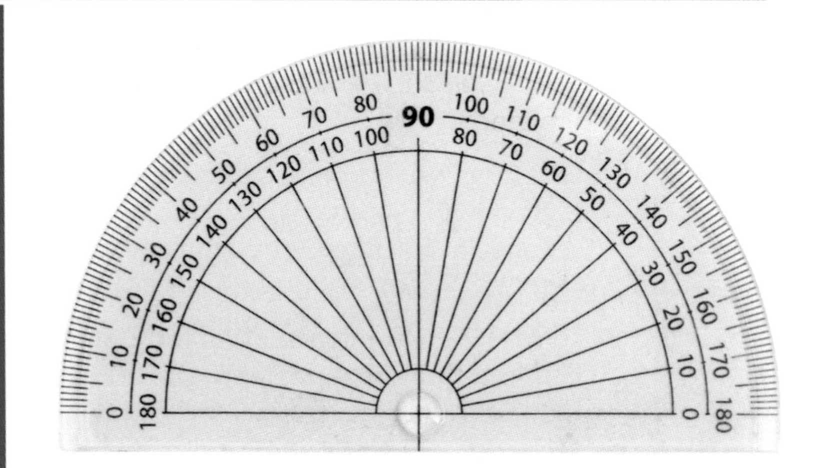

Step 1: Look at a protractor. Notice that a protractor has two scales. The outer one starts at zero on the left hand side, with a scale going up in a clockwise direction round to 180°. The inner scale starts on the right hand side, with a scale going up in an anti-clockwise direction round to 180°.

Step 2: Estimate first, is the angle acute or obtuse? This will give an idea of whether you are using the correct scale.

Step 3: Follow these guidelines:

- Line up the horizontal line of the protractor along one of the arms of the angle, as shown.
- Decide, do you have to move anti-clockwise or clockwise to get to the other arm of the angle? (In this case, anti-clockwise.)

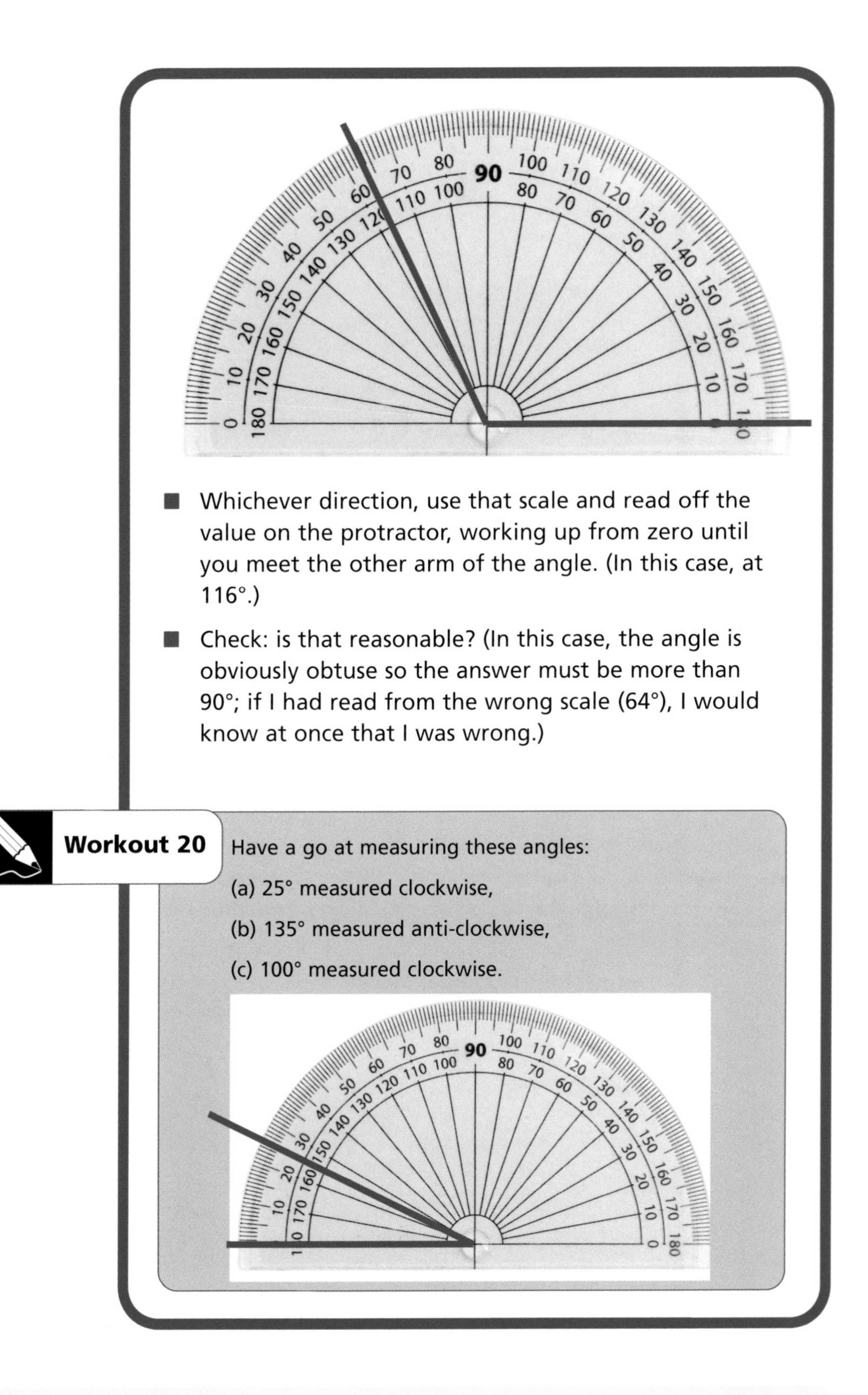

- Whichever direction, use that scale and read off the value on the protractor, working up from zero until you meet the other arm of the angle. (In this case, at 116°.)
- Check: is that reasonable? (In this case, the angle is obviously obtuse so the answer must be more than 90°; if I had read from the wrong scale (64°), I would know at once that I was wrong.)

Workout 20

Have a go at measuring these angles:

(a) 25° measured clockwise,

(b) 135° measured anti-clockwise,

(c) 100° measured clockwise.

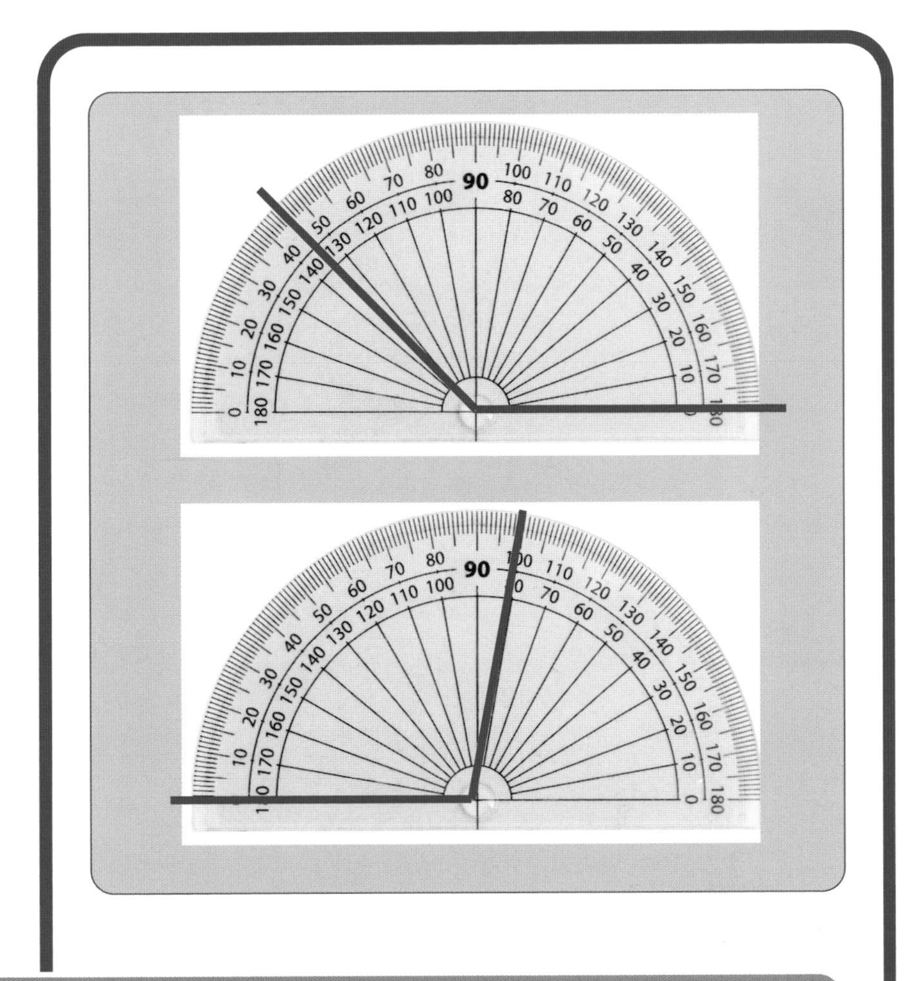

Calculating angles on a straight line

Knowing that angles on a straight line add up to 180° means that children can now solve geometrical problems involving this fact.

For example:

65° a°

(Not to scale)

Find the size of a°.

a° = 115°, as 65°+ a°= 180°

Since there are 360° in a full turn, children can also calculate angles at a point too.

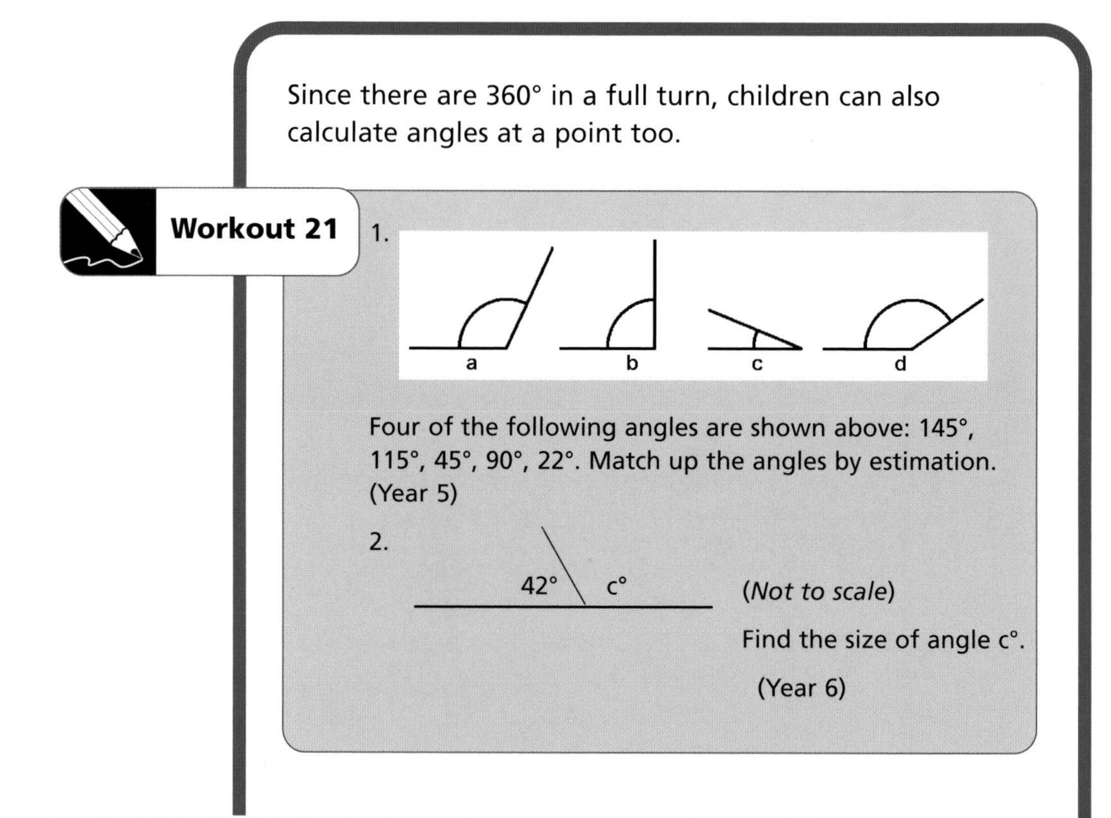

Workout 21

1. Four of the following angles are shown above: 145°, 115°, 45°, 90°, 22°. Match up the angles by estimation. (Year 5)

2. (*Not to scale*)

   Find the size of angle c°.

   (Year 6)

Angles in a triangle

As children progress through their primary maths education, they begin to appreciate more about properties of shapes. One property that is important is being able to calculate the size of individual angles in a 2-D shape.

The simplest shape is the triangle. Sometime, by about Year 6, most children learn that all the angles in a triangle add up to 180°. The actual proof of this comes much later on in their mathematical studies, but you can demonstrate an example of this very easily.

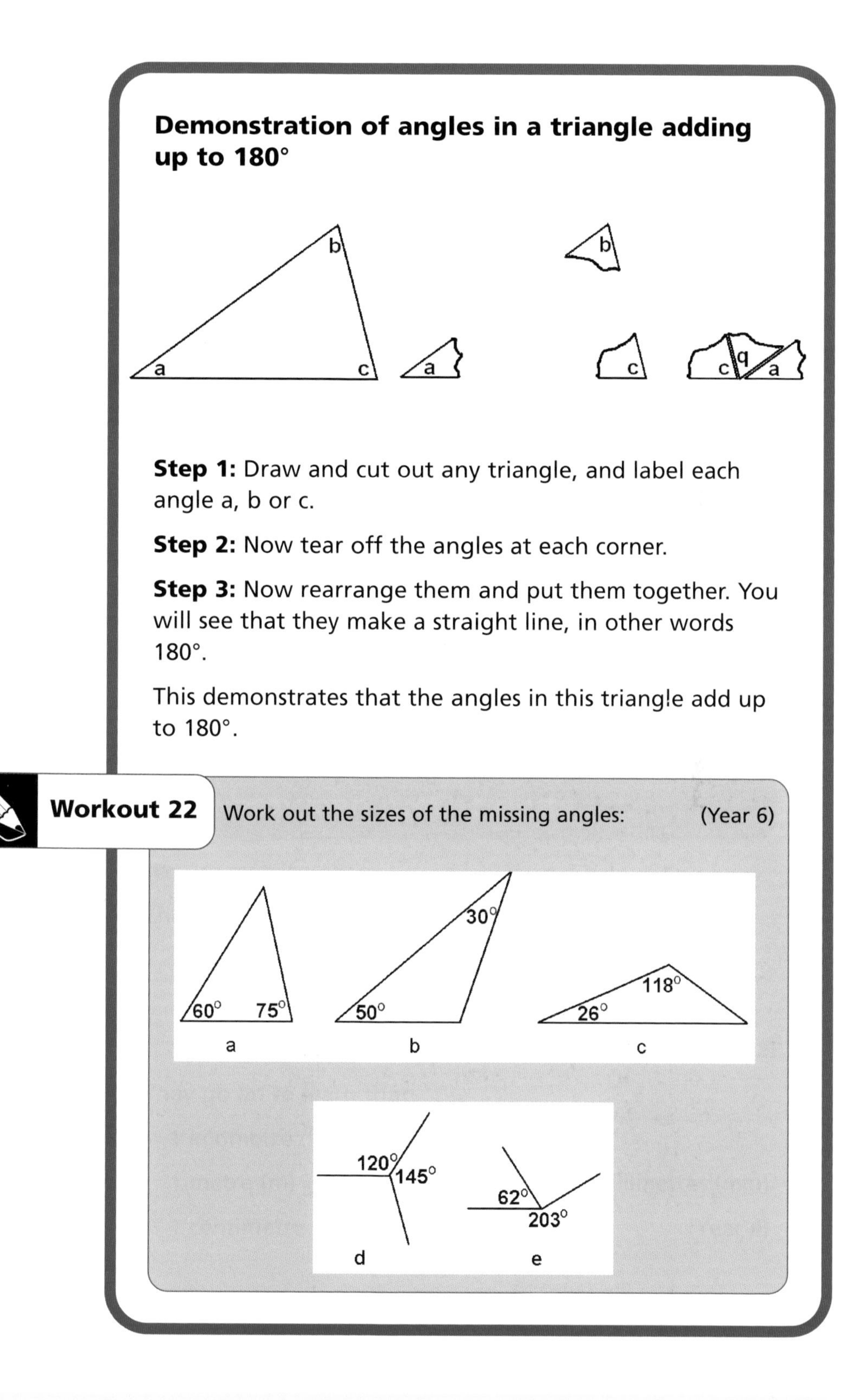

Demonstration of angles in a triangle adding up to 180°

Step 1: Draw and cut out any triangle, and label each angle a, b or c.

Step 2: Now tear off the angles at each corner.

Step 3: Now rearrange them and put them together. You will see that they make a straight line, in other words 180°.

This demonstrates that the angles in this triangle add up to 180°.

Workout 22 Work out the sizes of the missing angles: (Year 6)

How the concept of area is taught

To get over the notion of area being a measure of how much surface is covered, children would perhaps compare two shapes, and see which had the greatest area by covering each with, say, pennies. They then see which needed the greatest number of pennies, and so had the greatest area.

Children start learning about calculating area in Year 4.

Calculating areas of rectangles

What is the area of this rectangle?

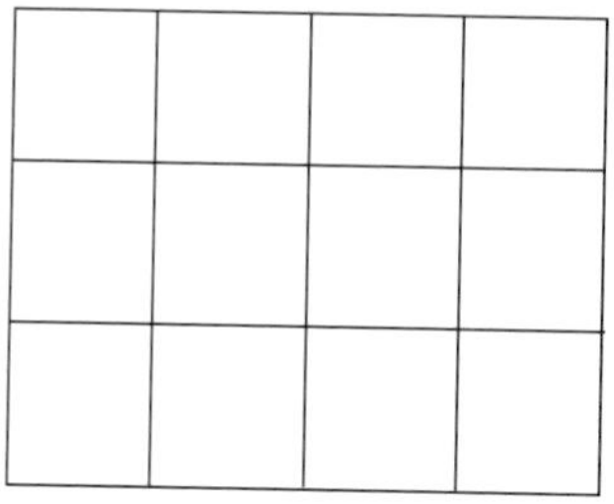

We can see, by counting the individual squares, that the area is 12 square centimetres, 12 cm^2.

However, the area can be calculated by seeing it as:

3 rows of 4 squares,

3 lots of 4 squares,

Or $3 \times 4 = 12$ squares.

Notice, this is the same as:

4 columns of 3 squares,

4 lots of 3 squares

Or $4 \times 3 = 12$ squares.

Notice this is the same as length × width (4×3).

The formula (rule) for calculating the area of a rectangle is:

Area of a rectangle = length × width

Use of formulae

We can shorten length to be l, width to be w and the area to be A, and write:

$A = l \times w$

Using letters like this, to represent numbers, is an example of a formula (plural: formulae), and a good example of algebra.

Children use formulae, first in words and then in letters, in about Year 5.

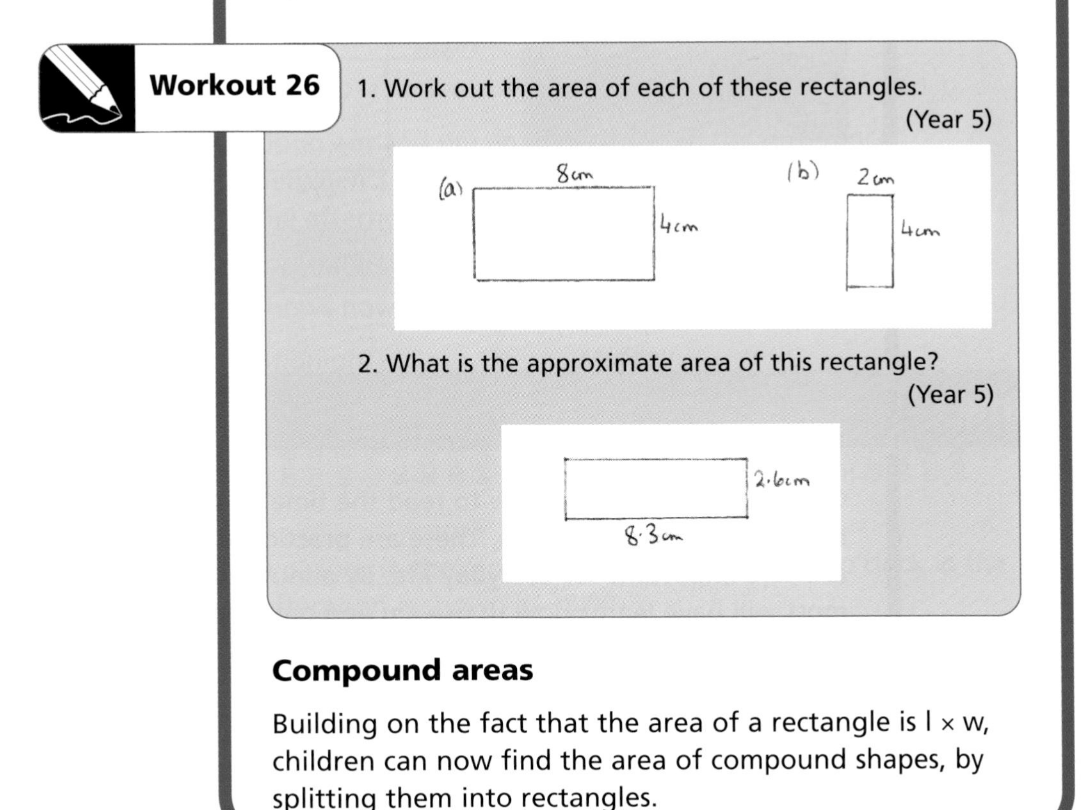

Workout 26

1. Work out the area of each of these rectangles. (Year 5)

2. What is the approximate area of this rectangle? (Year 5)

Compound areas

Building on the fact that the area of a rectangle is l × w, children can now find the area of compound shapes, by splitting them into rectangles.

In about Year 5 children start to calculate using the 24-hour clock.

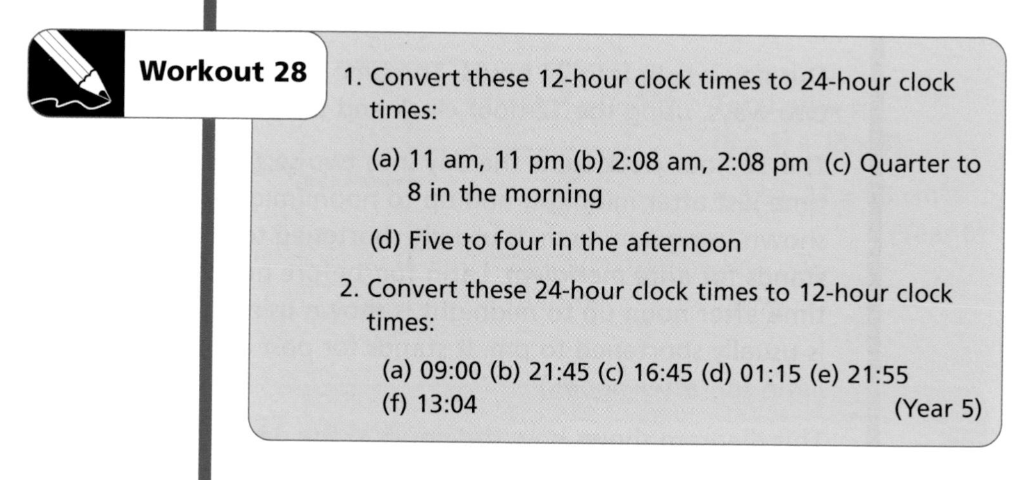

Workout 28

1. Convert these 12-hour clock times to 24-hour clock times:

   (a) 11 am, 11 pm (b) 2:08 am, 2:08 pm (c) Quarter to 8 in the morning

   (d) Five to four in the afternoon

2. Convert these 24-hour clock times to 12-hour clock times:

   (a) 09:00 (b) 21:45 (c) 16:45 (d) 01:15 (e) 21:55 (f) 13:04

(Year 5)

Lengths of journeys using 24-hour clock

It is important not only to be able to understand train and bus timetables so that we can plan when to arrive on time to catch the bus or train, but also to calculate how long journeys take. We need to be able to interpret the tables. These are everyday skills that parents can help with and support in a very practical way.

For example, imagine you are at a bus stop at 2:15 pm. The bus timetable shows that the times the bus stops there are:

9 am, 10 am, 11:30 am, 1 pm, 3 pm, 4:30 pm.

How long until the next bus? (Year 4)

Here, you need to recognize where your arrival at the bus stop fits in the schedule (between 1 pm and 3 pm).

You have missed the 1 pm, as 2:15 pm is after that time. So now count on until the next bus.

2:15 —(45 min)→ 3 pm. The answer is 45 minutes.

Mentally, we have been using what could be described as a timeline, very much like a number line, with hours marked off.

Here is another example using the 24-hour clock.

A train leaves at 14:35 and arrives at 17:10. How long does the journey take?

The best way to do this is to count on to 'landmark' times as shown, then total these times.

25 min + 2 hours + 10 min

14:35 ——→ 15:00 ——→ 17:00 ——→ 17:10

Total time = 25min + 2 hours + 10 min = 2 hours 35 minutes. (Year 5)

Workout 29

Using the timetable above, answer this question. If the 11:30 am bus is 15 minutes late, what time does it arrive? (Year 4)

How to help your child

Look at some train timetables and work out lengths of journeys, and times between each station (Year 5).

Plan an outing using trains and buses with your child. Have fun!

Handling data

Background

We make decisions all the time, often without consciously realizing it. For example, we make a decision to cross the road. We hardly notice that our decision is based on a number of factors. Is the road clear? Is this a safe place to see oncoming traffic? How far can we see? How fast does traffic move here? etc.

The process of sifting raw data, in this case the state of the traffic flow, to give us useful information (yes, it looks OK to cross), to making the final decision to cross the road is known as Data Handling.

Organizing the data into useful information so that decisions can be made is used in a number of professional situations. For example, in business the data about customers' shopping habits helps form the information needed to make decisions about what to stock, etc.

One way that helps us to organize data so that useful information can be seen is to put the data into tables or pie charts.

Average

It is useful to summarize data we have collected – to represent it as a typical value. One way we do this is to talk about 'the average'.

The range

It is also helpful to know the difference between the highest and lowest value. In other words, how spread out the data values are. The difference between the highest and lowest value is called 'the range'.

Types of averages

There are three types of averages: the mode, the median and the mean.

The mode

The mode is the value that occurs the most often. If we look at the number of goals scored by a football team in 11 matches:

1, 5, 2, 0, 7, 2, 1, 2, 6, 2, 5

the score that occurs the most often is 2, and so the mode is 2.

The range is 7 – 0 = 7

Children learn about finding the mode in Year 5. In about Year 6, they are introduced to the other two ways of giving an average.

The median

The median is the middle value, when we have rearranged the data, putting the values in order, starting with the lowest.

With our example above, when we put the values in order, we get:

Middle value – median

↓

0, 1, 1, 2, 2, **2**, 2, 5, 5, 6, 7

The median is 2, it is the middle value.

If we had an even number of values, the median is the middle two values added together, and divided by two. For example:

These are the two middle numbers.

↓ ↓

2, 3, 3, **4**, **5**, 7, 8, 9

The median in this case is = 4.5

The mean

The mean is found by adding together all the values, and then dividing the sum by the number of values.

In our example about the football scores, there were 11 scores, so we divide the total by 11.

$$\text{Mean} = \frac{0 + 1 + 1 + 2 + 2 + 2 + 2 + 5 + 5 + 6 + 7}{11} = \frac{33}{11} = 3$$

Notice that the mean, median and mode may take different values.

Workout 30

1. Here is a list of shoe sizes:

   Steve 5, Alf 4, Ali 5, James 6, Sean 3, Paul 5, Kristran 3.

   (a) (i) What is the range? (ii) What is the mode? (Year 5)

   (b) (i) Find the median and (ii) the mean. (Year 6)

Probability

When we talk about probability, we are generally discussing the likelihood of something taking place. It may come as a surprise to learn that we are all the time making decisions based on probability. For instance, we decide whether to take an umbrella depending on the likelihood of rain. We will often say, 'I think I'll chance it and not wear a coat.'

In these decisions, we are not only subconsciously working out the probability of something happening, but we are actively using it!

How is probability taught in schools?

In about Year 5, children are introduced to the topic of probability using language associated with probability to discuss events. Typical words associated with probability are: unlikely, likely, likelihood; certain, uncertain; fair, unfair; impossible, possible, probable; no chance, poor chance, good chance, certain.

We are mentally putting the likelihood of things occurring on a scale. Half way along is an even chance.

No chance | Even | Certainty

In about Year 6, children learn about events that are equally likely. For example, if we have a fair die (plural: dice), then each number is equally likely to occur when the die is rolled.

How to help your child

You can help by being aware of the language associated with probability and discussing events using the correct language.

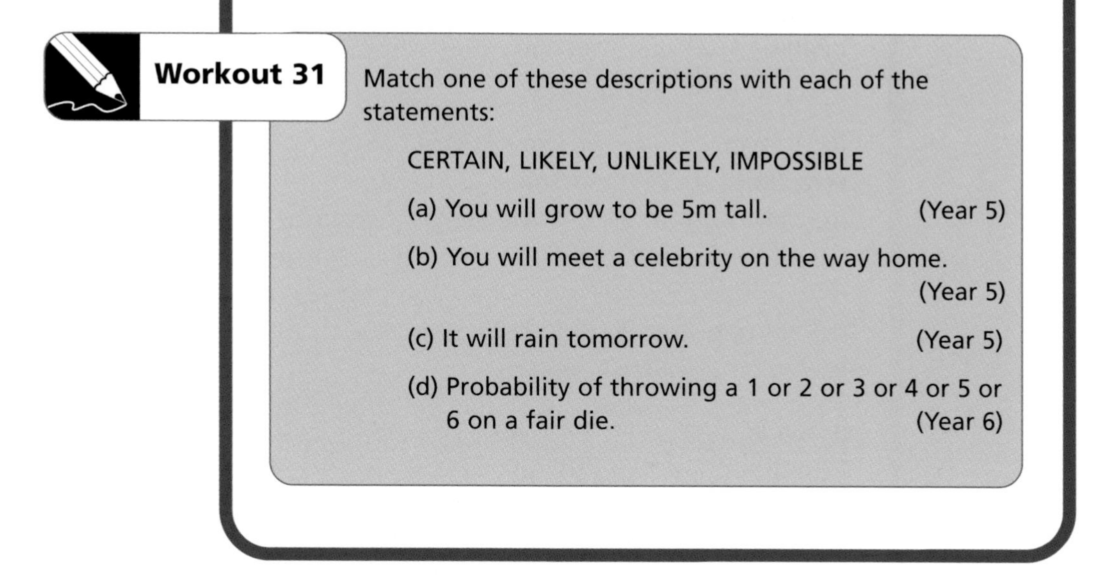

Workout 31

Match one of these descriptions with each of the statements:

CERTAIN, LIKELY, UNLIKELY, IMPOSSIBLE

(a) You will grow to be 5m tall. (Year 5)

(b) You will meet a celebrity on the way home. (Year 5)

(c) It will rain tomorrow. (Year 5)

(d) Probability of throwing a 1 or 2 or 3 or 4 or 5 or 6 on a fair die. (Year 6)

Glossary

Array

This is an organized arrangement of objects.

Average

An average is a way we summarize data to give a 'typical value'. There are three types of average, the mean, the median and the mode. (See below.)

Decimals or decimal fractions

Decimals, or decimal fractions to give them their full name, are fractions with denominators 10, 100, 1000, etc. We use a special notation to write these fractions, called decimal notation, and write

$$\frac{1}{10} \text{ as } 0.1, \ \frac{1}{100} \text{ as } 0.01, \text{ etc.}$$

Denominator

See fractions.

Fractions

In everyday life, we use the word fraction to mean something smaller. Fractions have a similar meaning in mathematics except that when you split something into fractions, either an item such as a cake, or an amount such as 30p, you split whatever you start with into smaller *equal* parts. Halving is splitting the something into two equal parts; splitting into thirds means splitting the something into three equal parts.

We use special symbols to show a fraction.

A half is written ½. The bottom number (the **denominator**) tells you the number of equal parts, the top number (the **numerator**) tells you the number of these equal parts you want.

Inverse operations

These are operations that reverse or 'undo' the original operation.

Division and multiplication are what are known as inverse operations. Addition and subtraction are also inverse operations.

E.g. With addition and subtraction, starting with 4, then *add* 3, we get 7. But, 7 *minus* 3 gets us back to 4, the number we started with. The subtraction undoes the addition.

Written out, it looks like this: $4 + 3 = 7$, and $7 - 3 = 4$.

The same happens with division and multiplication. If we start with 3 multiplied by 4 we get 12. If we divide 12 by 4 we get 3, the number we started with.

Written out, it looks like this: $3 \times 4 = 12$, and $12 \div 4 = 3$.

Mean

The mean is one of the ways we describe an average.

The mean is found by adding together all the values, and then dividing the sum by the number of values.

For example, find the mean of this club's football scores:

1, 5, 2, 0, 7, 2, 1, 2, 6, 2, 5

There were 11 scores, so we add together the scores, and divide the total by 11.

$$\text{Mean} = \frac{0 + 1 + 1 + 2 + 2 + 2 + 2 + 5 + 5 + 6 + 7}{11} = \frac{33}{11} = 3$$

Median

The median is one of the ways we describe an average. The median is the middle value, when we have rearranged the data, putting the values in order, starting with the lowest (see 'Handling data', *The median*).

Mode
The mode is one of the ways we describe an average. The mode is the value that occurs the most often. So if we look at the number of goals scored by a football team in 11 matches:

1, 5, 2, 0, 7, 2, 1, 2, 6, 2, 5

The score that occurs the most often is 2. And so the mode is 2.

Numerator
See fractions.

Partitioning
This is splitting a number into 100s, 10s and units etc. For example, twelve is a ten and a two, or 12 = 10 + 2.

Range
The range is the difference between the highest and lowest values in a set of data.

Ratio
A ratio is a way we compare two or more quantities. The list of ingredients for a recipe is an example of a practical way we use ratios.

Sequence
A sequence is a list of numbers (or shapes) that are in a given order, and there is a rule for continuing the sequence and finding the next member, and as many subsequent members as we may want to find.

Symbols
: We use a colon as the symbol to mean ratio.

> Means 'is greater than'. For example, 7 > 3, which says, '7 is greater than 3'. Please note, the larger number is at the wide side of the symbol, and the smaller number is at the pointed side of the symbol.

< Means 'is less than'. For example, 43 < 85, which says, '43 is less than 85'. Please note, the smaller number is at the pointed side of the symbol, and the larger number is at the wide side of the symbol.

Appendix 1: Multiplication square

Here is a multiplication square showing all the times tables up to 10 × 10.

×	1	2	3	4	5	6	7	8	9	10
1	1	2	3	4	5	6	7	8	9	10
2	2	4	6	8	10	12	14	16	18	20
3	3	6	9	12	15	18	21	24	27	30
4	4	8	12	16	20	24	28	32	36	40
5	5	10	15	20	25	30	35	40	45	50
6	6	12	18	24	30	36	42	48	54	60
7	7	14	21	28	35	42	49	56	63	70
8	8	16	24	32	40	48	56	64	72	80
9	9	18	27	36	45	54	63	72	81	90
10	10	20	30	40	50	60	70	80	90	100

Using the fact that multiplication and division are inverse operations, we can use the square to calculate divisions too.

Highlighted is:

3 × 4 = 12.

We can also use the same highlighted squares to work out that:

12 ÷ 4 = 3 and 12 ÷ 3 = 4.

Students use the square in this way in about Year 5.

Try using it for yourself to check your multiplication and division facts.

Appendix 2: Useful resources

Here are some useful resources that I can recommend, which can also be used to help your child with numeracy.

1. Some schools have been sending home Parent Booklets that give a list of numeracy targets for your child for the year, and give ideas of how to help your child with mathematics. You can download these for yourself at:

   http://www.standards.dfes.gov.uk/primary/publications/mathematics/12792/

2. The government has a very useful website for parents, which gives a list of the targets for your child in a number of subjects. You can see this at:

   http://www.parentscentre.gov.uk/learnjourn/index_ks2.cfm?ver=graph&subject=ma

   The government's Parents' Centre website also has lots of information about numeracy and other educational matters. You can see this at:

   http://www.parentscentre.gov.uk/educationandlearning/whatchildrenlearn/curriculumandassessment/

   The Department for Children, Schools and Families has produced some information for parents to help support their children in Year 5 and Year 6 with learning mathematics. You can see this at:

   http://www.standards.dfes.gov.uk/primary/publications/mathematics/pri_ma_hcm0014208/

3. The BBC has some very good numeracy games and activities that are suitable for supporting your child's work in maths. You can see these on their website:

   http://www.bbc.co.uk/schools/parents/search/

4. The Basic Skills Agency has some helpful publications for parents which can be downloaded. For example, their *Count and figure it out together* has some useful ideas for parents to support their children's learning about maths using everyday objects. See:

   http://archive.basic-skills.co.uk/resources/resourcessearchresults/detail.php?ResourceID=485287096

Appendix 3: Metric/Imperial conversions

Here is a table of approximate conversions between some commonly used metric and Imperial units.

1 litre	= 1¾ pints
4.5 litres	= 1 gallon or 8 pints
1 kilogram	= 2.2lb (pounds)
30g	= 1oz (ounce) (Some text books use 25g = 1oz)
8 km	= 5 miles

Appendix 4: Workout answers

Workout 1
(a) 23 (b) 48 (c) 81 tens

Workout 2
1. 4310
2. 70
3. 48
4. 4000
5. 0.73
6. 20

Workout 3
1. 35
2. 90
3. 340

Workout 4
1. 37, 32, 27
2. 31, 34, 37, 40, 43, 46, 49
3. Starting at –25, to find the next term add 3. Missing numbers are –16, –13, –10
4. Starting at 5, to find the next term add 14. The sequence is 5, 19, 33, 47, 61, 75, 89

Workout 5
1. (i) 0.6 (ii) 48.7
2. (i) 4.8kg is lighter
   (ii) 3.28kg is lighter
3. 8.92, 8.95, 8.98, 9.04, 9.09
4. £6.04 is less

Workout 6
1. (i) 5 (ii) 2 (iii) 8
2. (i) 21 (ii) 12 (iii) 27
3. 210cm

Workout 7
1. £35
2. 10% = £1.50, 20% = £3, 40% = £6
3. 50% = £12,000, 25% = £6000, 12½% = £3000

Workout 9
1. (a) 540 (b) 950
2. 400
3. 7000
4. 2200
5. (c)

Workout 12
1. £2.33
2. 1.7 litres or 1700ml

Workout 15
1. 265cm or 2.65m
2. £4.43

Workout 19
1. b, d, c, a
2. Acute: b, c, d, f. Obtuse: a, e

Workout 20
Read off the scales
(a) 25° (b) 135° (c) 100°

Workout 21
1. a = 115°, b = 90°, c = 22°, d = 145°
2. 138°

Workout 22
1. a = 45°, b = 100°, c = 36°, d = 95°, e = 95°

Workout 23

1. 3000g
2. 6000m
3. 50mm
4. 280cm
5. 1.7 litres
6. 0.55kg
7. 2350 ml

Workout 24

1. Your own answers
2. 8cm
3. 24cm

Workout 25

1. 38 cm

Workout 26

1. (a) 32 cm^2, (b) 8 cm^2
2. 24 cm^2

Workout 27

1. 36 cm^2
2. Your own answer

Workout 28

1. (a) 11:00, 23:00 (b) 02:08, 14:08 (c) 07:45 (d) 15:55
2. (a) 9 am (b) 9.45 pm (c) 4.45 pm (d) 1.15 am (e) 9.55 pm (f) 1.04 pm

Workout 29

1. 11.45 am

Workout 30

1. In order, the sizes are: 3, 3, 4, 5, 5, 5, 6
   (a) (i) 3 (ii) 5
   (b) (i) 5 (ii) $4\frac{3}{7}$

Workout 31

1. (a) Impossible (b) Own answer (c) Own answer (d) Certain